D1302806

WATER WONDERS of the WORLD

FROM KILLER WAVES TO MONSTERS OF THE DEEP

BY JANET NUZUM MYERS

For my parents, Edyth and Robert–J.N.M.

TEXT COPYRIGHT © 2007 by Janet Nuzum Myers

PHOTOGRAPHY AND ILLUSTRATION CREDITS:
Every effort has been made to trace the ownership of all copyright materials in this book and to obtain permission for their use.

Front cover (Niagara Falls): © Lisa Marzano/istockphoto.com; front cover (wave): © Paul Topp/istockphoto.com; front cover (shark): © Royalty-Free/CORBIS; front cover (ship), pp. 18, 20, 48, 69, 72 (inset) 75 (top), 78 (inset), 82: The Granger Collection, New York; back cover, pp. 8, 16, 26, 32, 40, 50, 56, 64, 72, 78, 86: © Monica Lau/Getty Images; pp. 4-5: © Will Evans/istockphoto.com; p. 6-7: © Radu Razvan/istockphoto.com; p. 9: © AP Photo/APTN; p. 10: © David Pu'u/CORBIS; pp. 12, 14, 15: Courtesy the National Oceanic and Atmospheric Administration/Department of Commerce; p. 17: © www.bridgda.com; p. 19: Rue des Archives/The Granger Collection, New York; pp. 24, 42: © Reuters/CORBIS; p. 28: © Peter Parks/Image Quest 3-D; p. 29: © Bryan C. Ladner; p. 31: © Bill Curtsinger/Getty Images; p. 32 (inset): Courtesy Yeorgos N. Lampathakis/National Geographic Society; p. 35: © Kenny Miller; p. 37: © Mel Fisher Maritime Heritage Society; p. 38: © Mel Fisher Maritime Heritage Society; p. 40 (inset): © The Mariners' Museum/CORBIS; pp. 43, 70, 86 (inset): © Bettmann/CORBIS; p. 46 (top): © Jeff Rotman/SeaPics.com; p. 46 (bottom): © Mark Conlin/SeaPics.com; p. 49: © AP Photo/HO, National Science Museum; p. 51: © Maximilian Weinzierl/Alamy Images; p. 52: © Anthony Bannister; Gallo Images/CORBIS; p. 53: © Astrid & Hanns Frieder-Michler/Science Photo Library/Photo Researchers, Inc.; p. 54: © Oliver Mackes/NicoleOttawa/Photo Researchers, Inc.; p. 57: © Jason Hawkes/CORBIS; p. 59: © Vo Trung Dung/CORBIS SYGMA; p. 60: © Colin McPherson/CORBIS SYGMA; p. 62: © Jon Jones/CORBIS SYGMA; p. 65: © Leonard de Selva/CORBIS; p. 66: © Charles E. Rotkin/CORBIS; p. 68: © William A. Bake/CORBIS; p. 71: © Kelly-Mooney Photography/CORBIS; p. 73: The Art Archive/Antiquarium Imera Sicily/Dagli Orti; p. 74: The Art Archive/Dagli Orti (A); p. 75 (bottom): © 2005 J.R. Robinson-Sideshowworld.com; p. 76: © Ben Cropp Productions/SeaPics.com; pp. 77, 90: © James D. Watt/SeaPics.com; p. 81 (top): © Hans Georg Roth/CORBIS; p. 81 (bottom): © Danny Lehman/CORBIS; p. 84: Ann Ronam Picture Library/HIP/Art Resource, NY; p. 85: © Segio Pitamitz/CORBIS; p. 87: © Masa Ushioda/SeaPics.com; p. 88: © Ron & Valerie Taylor/SeaPics.com; p. 91: © Doug Perrine/SeaPics.com; p. 92: © Richard Herrmann/SeaPics.com; p. 93: © David B. Fleetham/SeaPics.com

ALL RIGHTS RESERVED.

No part of this publication may be reproduced, except in the case of quotation for articles or reviews, or stored in any retrieval system, or transmitted in any form or by any means, electronic, mechanical, photocopying, recording, or otherwise, without written permission from the publisher.

FOR INFORMATION CONTACT:

MONDO Publishing
980 Avenue of the Americas
New York, NY 10018

Visit our web site at http://www.mondopub.com

Printed in China

07 08 09 10 11   9 8 7 6 5 4 3 2 1

ISBN 1-59336-729-5 (PB)

COVER AND BOOK DESIGN BY Michelle Farinella

Library of Congress Cataloging-in-Publication Data

Myers, Janet Nuzum, 1940-
  Water wonders of the world : from killer waves to monsters of the deep /
by Janet Myers.
      p. cm.
  Includes bibliographical references.
  ISBN 1-59336-729-5 (pbk.)
1. Oceanography--Juvenile literature. 2. Marine sciences--Juvenile
literature. I. Title.
  GC21.5.M94 2006
  910--dc22
              2005019792

CONTENTS

India

Sri Lanka

⋆ Phuket, Thailand

Indonesia

INDIAN
OCEAN

INTRODUCTION
~ WHAT ARE WATER WONDERS?

What are water wonders? A wonder is something that captures our attention. It surprises or mystifies us, or it leaves us awestruck. Our oceans and lakes are filled with such wonders. Some are natural wonders, like the ocean's incredible power. We are fascinated by underwater earthquakes that can generate deadly towering waves. Others consist of the creatures that live in lakes and oceans. Some are real, while others. . .well, you can read about them and then be the judge. Water wonders include strange places that exist in the seas and the mysterious events that occur there. Can they be explained?

Our big blue planet is about 70 percent water. Even today, with our twenty-first century technology, there's much we still do not know

Introduction

about Earth's oceans and lakes. The unknown can be scary, but it's also

captivating. It challenges us to be brave and to make possibly dangerous

explorations in an attempt to find answers. And even though the answers

may never be found, the hunt for them is often the most fascinating part.

Let's explore.

CHAPTER ONE
A Killer Wave Called Tsunami

It is Sunday, December 26, 2004. An early morning tropical sun blazes in the blue sky. The sea looks calm. But disaster is about to erupt in this area of the Indian Ocean.

Miles below the surface of the water, the ocean floor trembles. Suddenly, two massive rocky slabs in the earth's crust move and collide with a violent jolt. Seawater churns and swirls. Shock waves fan out from the powerful earthquake, which registers 9.0 on the Richter Scale. But up above, on the ocean's surface, the water level rises only slightly. A ship passes nearby, and the people on board notice nothing unusual.

Far below in the depths, the shock waves cause powerful waves of water to race out in all directions. The deep underwater waves reach a speed of over 500 miles per hour (805 km/hour). It's the strongest quake in 40 years, and it has set off what will be the deadliest tsunami (tsoo-NAH-mee) in recorded history.

In the tsunami's path lie several countries that border the Indian Ocean. Vacationers and villagers are unaware that a watery danger is rushing toward them. As the waves near the shore, they slow down and pile up, becoming one giant wave.

At some coastlines a strange thing happens: An odd hissing sound is heard. The water pulls back from the beach, toward the sea. A large area of the ocean floor is exposed. People on the beach stare at the weird sight. Stranded fish flop on the bare, wet sand. This is a red flag, a warning that something is terribly

Chapter ONE

wrong. "Run! Run!" someone shouts. But it's too late.

Here it comes! A terrifying wall of water, 30 feet (9.1 m) high, rushes ashore. The destruction is quick. Buildings, houses, and vehicles are crushed. Thousands of people drown. Floating debris rams into other victims, causing injury or death. A killer wave has struck, leaving behind devastation and misery.

Indonesia was hit first and hardest. There the tsunami took more than 100,000 lives, with over 120,000 more people missing and

This image, taken from an amateur video, shows the tsunami coming ashore on Sunday, December 26, 2004, in Phuket, Thailand.

presumed dead. Sri Lanka lost over 30,000 people. India, Thailand, and other countries also suffered casualties. The total death toll was estimated at a shocking 280,000. Dazed, grief-stricken survivors searched for missing family members and friends. A true death count was impossible because thousands of bodies were washed out to sea, and there was a lack of information from remote villages.

WHAT IS A TSUNAMI?

How could so many people be caught by surprise? And why wasn't the earthquake noticed by people on the ship? To answer questions like these, we must understand what a tsunami is and how it works.

Normal waves are formed by winds blowing across the ocean's surface. A tsunami is not a normal wave. The word *tsunami* is a Japanese word meaning "harbor wave." It can be one wave or a group of waves. A tsunami is often called a tidal wave, although the tides are not what cause it to occur.

How does it begin? A tsunami can be triggered by a volcano or a landslide either in or near the water. However, a strong ocean-bottom earthquake is usually the cause. If you toss a pebble into a pond, you've disturbed the water. From the pebble's entry spot, small waves of water ripple away in widening circles. Now imagine the disturbance caused by a big underwater earthquake. Compared to the pebble's ripples, a quake's ripples, or waves, are millions of times more powerful. They surge in all directions. The deeper the ocean, the faster the waves move. In deep water a tsunami can race as fast as a jet airplane, over 500 miles per hour (805 km/hour), and it can travel for thousands of miles.

While this is happening far below, the surface waves of the open sea might rise only a few feet, and are easily overlooked. But when the waves move from the deep ocean to the shallow water near a coastline, they change. As if putting on the brakes, the ocean bottom slows down the waves, and they merge to become one huge wave. Some waves rise over 100 feet (30.5 m)—as high as a 10-story building—before crashing on shore. Not all tsunamis are that monstrous. The December 2004 tsunami proved that even 30-foot (9.1-m) waves can be devastating.

How is a tsunami's height measured? After it has hit, scientists examine where debris is found and where trees and plants are dying from being water-logged with salty seawater. This tells them how high the wave must have been to cause the damage.

THE RING OF FIRE

Historically, the largest number of tsunamis have occurred in the area of the Pacific Ocean called the "Ring of Fire," which is a zone of active earthquakes and volcanoes. The December 2004 earthquake, however, was located at the outer edge of the ring, and affected countries around the Indian Ocean. Under both oceans lie restless tectonic (tek-TOHN-ik) plates, and this is where the trouble begins.

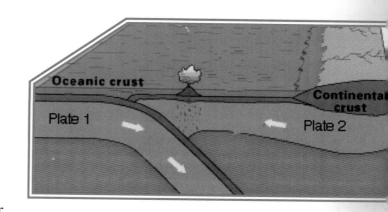

Plate tectonics

Tectonic plates are the huge slabs of rock that make up Earth's crust. At least seven large plates, and twelve smaller ones, cover our planet. Some are up to 80 miles (129 km) thick. They float on the molten rock of the asthenosphere (uh-STHEN-uh-sfeer). The edges of the plates move and bump against one another. Pressure builds up. The stress is finally released by a sudden break in the crust: an earthquake. Molten rock and gases escape from under the plates through volcanoes, which are vents in the crust. Like an earthquake a volcano can erupt either on dry land or under the ocean.

Along with its earthquakes and volcanoes, the Ring of Fire has something else that tsunamis need: extremely deep waters. Some of the deepest places in the world lie in the Pacific Ocean. For example, the Mariana Trench, at more than 36,000 feet (10,973 m), is so deep that it could hold Earth's highest mountain, Mount Everest, with almost another 7,000 feet (2,134 m) of ocean on top of it!

Earthquakes set off up to 95 percent of all tsunamis. But it was a volcano that started another destructive tsunami in the Indonesian area. In 1883, a small, bare, rocky island called Krakatoa (krak-uh-TOW-uh) sat quietly between the larger islands of Sumatra and Java. Krakatoa had a large volcano that rumbled to life and blew. The volcanic island crumbled into the water in a series of ear-splitting explosions, which could be heard as far away as Australia, about 2,200 miles (3,540 km) away. Enormous walls of water swept over the neighboring islands. More than 36,000 people drowned.

Near the center of the Ring of Fire, in the Pacific Ocean, lie the Hawaiian Islands. April Fool's Day in 1946 was a memorable day in Hawaii. The trouble began far away, with an ocean-bottom earthquake off the coast of Alaska. In the nearby Aleutian (uh-LOO-shun) Islands, five men on duty in a lighthouse drowned when a huge wave swallowed them up. From there the killer wave moved south toward Hawaii, where it arrived five hours later.

Tsunami hitting a pier in Hilo Harbor, Hawaii, on April 1, 1946. Notice the person standing on the pier (near left edge of photo).

Hilo, Hawaii, was hardest hit. One survivor later said, ". . . the bare sea floor was suddenly exposed, and people rushed down to the water's edge to pick up dying fish. Some people knew this meant a big wave was coming. 'Get to high ground!' someone yelled." Many who heard the warnings thought was an April Fool's Day joke, but it was no joke. The tsunami killed 159 people in Hawaii.

After this event the Pacific Tsunami Warning System was established in

Chapter ONE

Honolulu. When disturbances that could cause a tsunami were picked up, sirens warned people to watch out. But there was a problem. Not all earthquakes triggered tsunamis, and often the waves rolled in smaller than predicted. False alarms sounded so many times that people soon ignored the sirens. Unfortunately, this led to disaster.

In 1960, severe earthquakes jolted the Pacific Ocean floor near Chile, in South America. The ocean gushed with waves that wrecked villages, drowning about 1,500 people. Then the tsunami traveled west to Hawaii. It took about 15 hours for the brutal waves to cross the ocean. Sirens wailed in Hilo, Hawaii, one of the towns hit by the 1946 tsunami. But after years of false alarms, not everyone obeyed the warnings. Some people actually went to the beach to watch the waves come in!

The first two waves to reach Hilo were harmless. Then the third wave roared in at a height of 30 feet (9.1 m). Buildings fell and houses tumbled off foundations and floated out to sea. The rushing water smashed boats and tossed cars around like toys. Sixty-one people died from the tsunami's shattering power. The tsunami was not finished, however. About six hours later, it reached Japan, claiming 200 more lives and washing away some 5,000 homes.

Four years later, in 1964, one of the strongest earthquakes ever recorded (9.2) shook parts of Alaska. One newspaper writer claimed that when he tried to walk, it was like ". . .marching across a field of Jell-O®." Tall buildings collapsed, and 117 Alaskans were killed. Tons of earth along the Alaskan coastline fell into the sea, creating massive waves. The tsunami raced down the west coast of North America. Eleven more people died in California.

This tragedy led to the opening of another Tsunami Warning Center in Palmer, Alaska. Like Honolulu's center, its purpose is to watch for possible tsunamis. After the epicenter, or central point, of a severe earthquake is located, observation posts in countries throughout the Pacific are warned. Observers then decide if conditions are right for a tsunami, and they predict where it will strike and when it will arrive. Sirens, TV, and radio warnings tell people that a

Destruction from the 1964 tsunami in Kodiak, Alaska

tsunami is on the way.

Tragically, in December 2004, no such system was in place around the Indian Ocean. People were unaware of the killer waves rushing toward their coasts. A long-overdue tsunami warning system might have reduced the widespread death and damage.

DART (DEEP-OCEAN ASSESSMENT AND REPORTING OF TSUNAMIS)

Scientists are constantly improving the way tsunamis are forecast. In the United States, the National Oceanic and Atmospheric Administration (NOAA) runs a project called DART (Deep-ocean Assessment and Reporting of Tsunamis). DART works through a system of special buoys that float in the Pacific Ocean. After an earthquake, sensing devices on the seafloor determine the size of each wave and transmit the data to a surface buoy. Information from the buoy is relayed to a satellite. Then, from the satellite, the facts are beamed to the land-based warning centers. DART's fast and accurate information protects coastal communities and prevents false alarms.

On average, only one or two small tsunamis are reported each year. A big destructive tsunami usually comes around only once every 15 years. But in the 1990s, tsunamis were reported more often. They struck in more than five different years, in the western edge of the Pacific Rim (countries bordering the Pacific Ocean). About 4,800 lives were lost. Then came the 2004 Indian Ocean tsunami, which broke all records for death and destruction. Even though tsunamis seem to have been increasing, they are still quite rare, which is why they are among the least understood of Earth's natural disasters.

Sometimes it takes a stunning tragedy such as the tsunami of December 26, 2004, to spur changes. It focused attention on the need for warning systems in unprotected regions. Countries around the Indian Ocean that were devastated by the tsunami have begun developing their own warning systems. Hopefully, future disasters will be prevented. We cannot stop nature's violence, but we must keep looking for ways to protect people from it.

DART buoy in the ocean

The Pacific and Indian Oceans have the Ring of Fire, but the Atlantic Ocean has other dangers. Within the waters of the Atlantic lies a justly famous triangle-shaped region. Its fame comes from the dozens of tragedies and mysterious events that have occurred there. Many people consider the place cursed. . . .

CHAPTER TWO
❧ The Big, Bad Bermuda Triangle

According to an old saying, "It's hard to get rid of a bad reputation." Maybe that's the only thing wrong with the Bermuda Triangle—the place just has a bad reputation. Deserved or not, some people call this area of the Atlantic Ocean the "Devil's Triangle" or the "Triangle of Death."

To find this mysterious place, draw a triangle connecting the island of Bermuda, the island of Puerto Rico (PWERT-oh REE-coh), and Miami, Florida. Inside this triangle is a region of the Atlantic Ocean where scary things supposedly happen. What gives this place its reputation as a zone of doom?

THE TRIANGLE'S HISTORY

About five hundred years ago, the waters now called the Bermuda Triangle grabbed the attention of Christopher Columbus and his ship's crew while they were sailing through. Nervous sailors watched an orange fireball streak across the clear sky. One night they viewed bright lights flickering in the distance, although they were far from land. Another time the ship's compass began to act strangely. Then Columbus and his men spotted "glowing streaks of white water." Oddly, five centuries later, astronauts orbiting Earth mentioned seeing "glowing waters" in the same vicinity.

Most people hadn't heard of the Bermuda Triangle until about 40 years ago. Around that time several Florida newspapers published a list of unexplained disappearances off the southeastern coast of the United States. That's all it took

❧

for people to take a closer look. In 1964, a magazine article entitled "The Deadly Bermuda Triangle" was published. The author, Vincent Gaddis, had given the area a name that stuck. Gaddis pointed out that odd things were happening that seemed to go "beyond the laws of chance."

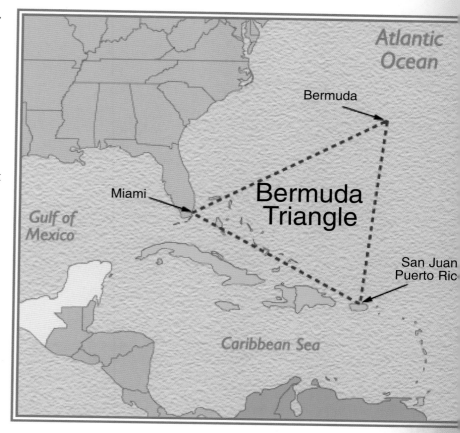

Interest grew, and other writers wondered about the mystery. Some of them expanded the boundaries of the Triangle to include the eerie Sargasso Sea. (More about the Sargasso Sea in the next chapter.) Over the years more than 100 ships and air-planes have vanished in the Triangle. At least 1,500 lives have been lost. And in most of these cases, an SOS, or a signal of distress, was not sent out. Search parties usually found nothing—no wreckage (not even oil slicks), no survivors, no bodies. Even more baffling is that many of the disappearances occurred during good weather and for no apparent reason.

SOME STRANGE EVENTS

Of all the Bermuda Triangle incidents, several stand out as especially puzzling. In the 1800s, deserted vessels were found drifting in the Triangle. A French ship, the *Rosalie*, was adrift with its sails set, carrying a full cargo.

An old painting of a ship caught in a storm in the Bermuda Triangle, in 1855

Where was the crew? They were never accounted for. Another time a United States sailing ship, the *James B. Chester*, was found bobbing on the sea. Again, the crew was missing, never to be found.

Even more curious is the story of an American ship, the *Ellen Austin*. The year was 1881. Off the coast of Bermuda, the ship came across a drifting schooner with no one on board. The captain of the *Ellen Austin* ordered his sailors to investigate. They found everything in place on the abandoned ship, including a valuable cargo of mahogany wood. The captain picked some men from his own crew to sail the schooner to port, escorted by the *Ellen Austin*.

During the voyage a raging storm separated the two ships. The schooner was sighted the next day, but the *Ellen Austin*'s captain and crew were startled to discover that the ship was again deserted. Two crews had evaporated into thin air! The *Ellen Austin* sailed quickly away from the deserted ship.

The USS Cyclops, *a Navy ship, disappeared in 1918.*

Another disappearance in the Bermuda Triangle left even more unanswered questions. In 1918, a huge Navy supply ship, the USS *Cyclops* (SYE-klops), sailed from the West Indies toward Virginia. A radio message from the *Cyclops* reported fair weather and no problems. That was the last contact from the 542-foot (165-m) ship and its 309 men. It simply disappeared. Searchers found nothing. How could a ship almost as long as two football fields vanish without a trace?

One of the most famous stories about the Bermuda Triangle is the saga of Flight 19, also known as the "Lost Patrol." Different versions have been told of

United States Navy Avenger torpedo bombers like these made up Flight 19 in 1945. All five planes were lost.

this doomed flight, but this one is based on the military's Official Board of Inquiry. Five United States Navy torpedo bombers left their base in Fort Lauderdale, Florida, in December 1945. The time was 2:10 P.M. The five planes carried a total of 14 airmen. The weather was good, and the sea was a little rough. The airmen turned east for a routine training flight over the Atlantic Ocean. At least, it was supposed to be routine.

Less than two hours after taking off, trouble began. The flight leader, Lieutenant Charles Taylor, radioed this message to the base: "Both my compasses are out, and I'm trying to find Fort Lauderdale, Florida. I'm over land. . . . I'm sure I'm in the Keys, but I don't know how far down, and I don't know how to get to Fort Lauderdale." The lieutenant sounded rattled.

Chapter TWO

Lieutenant Taylor was directed to put the sun on his port (left) wing and fly up the coast. Air traffic controllers were puzzled as to why the squadron needed to be told something so basic. Minutes later the lead pilot reported, "We have just passed over a small island. We have no other land in sight." How could they have run out of islands if they were flying north over the Florida Keys?

Over the next few hours, ground controllers tried to pinpoint the location of Flight 19, but they were unable to pick up the lost flight on radar. Static interfered with their messages. Bits of radioed transmissions added to the confusion. The planes flew a zigzag course without recognizing any landmarks. Flight 19 was hopelessly lost. How could five pilots have become so disoriented?

The squadron's final message came in at 6:20 P.M. "All planes close up tight. . .we'll have to ditch unless landfall. . .when the first plane drops below 10 gallons, we all go down together." After this there was only silence. Large search and rescue planes took off to find Flight 19, and within minutes another emergency arose. One of the rescue airplanes, carrying a crew of 13, disappeared, too.

It's possible that the rescue plane exploded suddenly. Witnesses on a tanker cruising off the Florida coast saw a burst of flames in the distance. They believed it to be a burning airplane plunging into the ocean. No one knew why the airplane exploded without any warning. Hundreds of ships and aircraft conducted a massive search for the total of 6 lost planes and 27 missing men. But neither wreckage nor bodies were found. The disasters still remain a mystery.

Incidents like these add to the Bermuda Triangle's reputation. Case after case can be cited where people say that "something weird is going on." Ships and planes of all sizes have disappeared, along with the people on them, but other people have lived to tell about their experiences. In 1966, a tugboat pulling a barge left Puerto Rico. The weather was clear. Suddenly they were surrounded by a strange, thick fog.

Twenty years later, in 1986, an airplane bound for Florida had a similar fog experience. During both incidents, when the vessels were covered by yellowish fog, instruments went crazy and radio contacts were lost. The bank of fog seemed to fight for control over the vessels. All at once the fog let them go. The yellow haze dissolved and the weather was clear again.

SOME OF THE THEORIES

Over the years strange events in the Bermuda Triangle have sparked debates. Even when the occurrences are explained, the answers do not satisfy everyone. Opinions range from those based on scientific facts to those that come from overactive imaginations. Some people suggest that supernatural forces are responsible. There are frequent reported UFO sightings in the region, and some believers suggest that a meeting place for aliens exists below the Triangle's surface. The disappearances, they say, are due to aliens kidnapping people in order to study them.

Another theory is that the lost island of Atlantis sank in the Triangle. (More about Atlantis in Chapter 10.) The idea is that crystals used by the people of Atlantis for power are underwater and still giving off energy. It is suggested that this energy is what causes instruments to fail in ships and airplanes. Other strange theories include time warps, parallel universes, even sea monsters.

But most people are skeptical of these unlikely theories. The doubters believe that the mysterious events that have occurred in the Bermuda Triangle are not mysteries at all. They believe that each incident can be explained. Likely causes include human error, equipment problems, or unpredictable and sometimes violent weather. Wild weather is common in the Atlantic Ocean. Far from shore, high winds turn choppy waves into monstrous towers of water that sink small boats. Dangerous whirling waterspouts, which look like tornadoes, form over the water.

Other natural phenomena can cause trouble for a ship as well. Deadly ocean whirlpools, called eddies, swirl on or below the sea's surface. Dangerous currents flow in the Atlantic Ocean, and the Gulf Stream sweeps through it like a powerful river. Deep trenches cut through the seafloor. The rough ocean could quickly suck down wreckage and bodies.

Skeptics also have explanations for disappearing airplanes. Microbursts, which are strong downdrafts of air, create wind gusts. Striking without warning, these powerful gusts can tear apart an airplane. Another explanation is that airplanes could explode due to fumes from fuel leaks suddenly igniting.

Still another theory involves large pockets of natural gas that lie beneath the ocean floor. The idea is that an earthquake releases a large amount of the natural gas, which bubbles up through the water and bursts into the air. A cloud of gas then forms, enveloping a low-flying airplane. The plane's engines stall, and the aircraft falls into the sea. Could the "glowing waters" seen from the sky be the natural gas bubbling to the surface of the ocean?

Then there are the instrument problems. The Bermuda Triangle is one of two regions in the world where a compass points toward true north. Normally a compass points to magnetic north. The difference between the two is called a "compass variation." Sailors and pilots must take this into account or they will go off course and become lost. Perhaps this could have something to do with the many disappearances.

Today air and sea traffic is heavy in the Bermuda Triangle. It's true that lives are sometimes lost there, but accidents occur in all of the world's oceans. The reality is that thousands of people safely travel through the Bermuda Triangle each day. Most people laugh at the names given to the Triangle, like the "Limbo of Lost Souls," or "Atlantic's Graveyard."

They believe these names make the area seem more dangerous than it really is. Respect the environmental dangers, they say, but don't believe the false notions that it's an evil, "jinxed" place. The truth is, the Bermuda Triangle is nothing to fear.

A waterspout is like a tornado over water.

Chapter TWO

The Bermuda Triangle reaches into a fascinating but unfamiliar section of the North Atlantic Ocean. Long ago, sailors would tremble with fright when forced to cross this strange sea that lies within the ocean. What is this frightening body of water?

CHAPTER THREE

Where in the World Is the Sargasso Sea?

Most people haven't even heard of the Sargasso Sea.

Sailors, however, have been aware of this body of water for centuries.

Go back in time 500 years. Imagine you are sailing on a big ship from Europe to the New World. Your ship's tall white sails are swelled with winds that push your vessel across the wide ocean. You and your shipmates are superstitious and worry about what lies ahead.

After weeks of travel, you awake one morning to a strange sensation. The ship isn't moving—it's becalmed. Limp sails prove that no breezes blow. Besides the still, heavy air, you notice another odd thing. The gently swelling water is crammed with floating clumps of yellow-brown seaweed. In the distance you see an island—but then you realize that it's not an island after all. It's a massive patch of the same strange seaweed.

A knot of fear twists in your stomach. You've heard frightful tales about these spooky ocean waters from sailors who journeyed here earlier. Seafarers told of vessels being captured forever by tentacles of seaweed. Others suggested that evil sea monsters lurked beneath the weedy clumps, waiting for victims to glide by. Huge whirlpools were reported to pull doomed ships to a watery grave at the bottom of the ocean.

Anxiety builds among you and your shipmates during hours of aimless drifting. Suddenly the winds return to puff up sagging sails. Relief calms your fear. The ship pushes westward, beyond the grasp of the tangled seaweed. What is this weird place? For hundreds of years, sailors have spread rumors and legends about this unique body of water that's a part of the North Atlantic Ocean.

One of the first written descriptions of this sea came from Christopher Columbus during his famous voyage of 1492. Because seaweed usually collects near coastlines, Columbus thought he was near land when his crew spotted the seaweed. They measured the depth of the water and were surprised to discover they were nowhere near land.

Columbus noted in his ship's log that for a few days, his three vessels sat nearly motionless. His crew became restless and nervous. Columbus worried that their food and water would run out, but the ships slowly drifted into the trade winds, and their voyage continued.

WHAT IS THE SARGASSO SEA?

Travelers sailing through this mysterious place often are fascinated by the masses of seaweed. A close look at the plants reveals that they are not a common variety. Feathery leaves grow on stems supported by small clumps of grape-like air sacs. The rootless seaweed reproduces when branch tips that break off and float away grow into new plants.

Sailors from Portugal named the plants *salgazo*, which means "little grapes." This sea of grapes eventually became known as the Sargasso Sea, and the floating plants were called sargassum (sahr-GAS-um). The mustard-color sargassum is usually thinly scattered across the water. But sometimes an amazing thing happens. Winds and currents cause the sargassum to line up in neat rows. Like orderly soldiers, the lines stretch several miles in length, making the water difficult for small craft to navigate.

Only in the last 50 years have oceanographers closely studied this peculiar place. They've found out the basics, like how big the Sargasso Sea is and where it's located. The sea is oval and is about 2,000 miles long and 700 miles wide (3,220 km by 1,127 km)—more than half the size of the continental United

Sargassum has yellowish, grapelike air sacs.

States. The exact location of the Sargasso Sea is hard to pinpoint since it constantly moves and has no land borders. It lies toward the middle of the North Atlantic Ocean and surrounds the island of Bermuda.

Reaching into the notorious Bermuda Triangle hasn't helped the Sargasso Sea's questionable reputation. But what makes the Sargasso Sea a separate and special place? Think of it as a huge bowl of warm water surrounded by the colder North Atlantic Ocean. Flowing around the Sargasso Sea are the fast moving currents of the Gulf Stream, racing in a clockwise direction like a gigantic wheel. Within this rotating ring, the Sargasso's waters are quiet, clear, and very salty. The region has less rain and wind, and fewer clouds than other parts of the ocean. These conditions are the reason for its nickname: "desert ocean."

Large clumps of sargassum in the Sargasso Sea

Sometimes the center section of the calm sea is a harsh reminder of human carelessness. Bottles, cans, chunks of wood, and other trash bob in the gentle swells as a kind of floating junkyard. Blobs of oil that have leaked from ships add to the shocking mess.

WHAT LIVES IN THE SARGASSO SEA?

Away from this gloomy inner area, the Sargasso Sea provides homes for many aquatic creatures; thousands of eels and sea turtles have thrived in the warm, calm waters. In the past, marine biologists weren't sure where European and American eels migrated to mate, but it's now known that the eels swim from opposite sides of the Atlantic Ocean to meet in the Sargasso Sea. They mate, lay their eggs, and then die. Soon a new generation of eels starts the long migration home.

Baby sea turtles also puzzled scientists until recently. Female sea turtles deposit their eggs along beaches in the southern United States, Central America, and the Caribbean Islands. After emerging from the eggs, the half-dollar-sized hatchlings scurry into the ocean and swim off. Biologists have discovered that many of these baby turtles somehow find their way to the Sargasso Sea. Here they feast on the barnacles, crabs, shrimp, and fish that live among the sargassum. Then, when they have grown large enough to defend themselves, the sea turtles return to open waters.

In recent years scientists have learned much about the unusual Sargasso Sea. Once feared, its reputation has gradually changed. The Sargasso is certainly a strange place, but it no longer contains secrets that add to the mystery. The lack of land borders makes this watery desert a challenge to study, but ongoing research will continue to increase our understanding of this sea within an ocean.

Chapter THREE

The Sargasso Sea hasn't claimed any treasure ships, as far as we know. But in other places, the wreckage of ships that once carried dazzling riches litters the ocean floor. Treasures wait to be found. . . .

Baby turtles scurry down the beach toward the ocean.

CHAPTER FOUR
~ Sunken Treasure Ship: The *Atocha*

In 1492, Spain sent Christopher Columbus on an expedition to find riches. He found much more than that—a part of the world Europeans didn't know existed, which they called the New World. Many expeditions followed. Spanish explorers soon conquered the mighty Aztec empire, claiming the Aztec's gold and their land. By the early 1600s, Spanish colonies were scattered among the Caribbean Islands, Mexico, Central America, and South America. Some settlers grew sugarcane, coffee, and cotton. Others mined vast amounts of silver, gold, and emeralds. The riches found in the New World made Spain a superpower in Europe. But Spain needed more and more gold to pay for its king's costly wars and lavish spending.

The *Atocha*

Twice a year, a fleet of Spanish merchant ships made the trip from Spain to the colonies. Leaving Spain, the ships carried supplies for the colonists. On the return voyage, however, the cargo was quite different. The ships were loaded with a seemingly endless array of riches that flowed from the New World. The Spanish government sent along heavily armed escort ships to guard the merchant vessels. In return, merchants paid a 20 percent tax on their cargo. Among the ships that left Havana in 1622 was one of Spain's newest escort ships, the *Atocha*.

~

Chapter FOUR

The 110-foot (33.5-m) long *Atocha* was a galleon (GAL-ee-un). Its three tall masts were rigged with square sails. Armed with 20 cannons, the special warship carried both cargo and passengers. Another galleon, the *Santa Margarita*, was also heavily armed. Because of their protection, both galleons were entrusted with the most valuable treasures. On board the *Atocha* were 265 people consisting of the crew, soldiers, and wealthy passengers. The largest ship was positioned at the end of the convoy so it could watch over the other vessels.

On September 4, the Spanish fleet, including the *Atocha* and the *Santa Margarita*, were preparing to leave Havana, Cuba, for the trip home to Spain. The ships were about six weeks behind schedule, and hurricane season had arrived. The crew were grumbling, worried about the late start. They knew that the route home was full of risks. Dangerous reefs lurked beneath shallow waters of the nearby coastlines. Some sailors feared possible attacks by English, French, or Dutch warships—enemies who were aware of the riches onboard the Spanish ships. There was also the threat of pirates—sea robbers who would steal from anyone.

Under clear skies the ships left Havana. The convoy had only managed to get as far as the Florida Keys (a cluster of islands extending out from the southwestern tip of Florida) before disaster struck. On the second day of the voyage, a violent hurricane moved in. All day and night the storm battered the helpless ships, pushing them into shallow water, and damage was widespread. After being bashed against a reef, the *Atocha* broke apart and sank. Within two days, eight of the ships had been destroyed. Hundreds of people had died. Gold, silver, emeralds, and jewelry had sunk to the ocean floor.

The next day rescuers found only five survivors clinging to the wreckage. Seven other ships had also sunk, including the *Santa Margarita*. The remaining 20 ships limped back to Havana for repairs and to report the disaster. Gone were eight ships, their precious cargo, and about 550 lives.

Desperate, the debt-ridden Spanish government sent salvage teams to look for the lost valuables. Much of the *Santa Margarita*'s treasure was recovered. But where was the *Atocha*? Not long after the first storm, a second hurricane washed away all traces of the massive galleon. Several searches turned up nothing. After a while the *Atocha* was forgotten, and it remained that way for more than 300 years.

MEL FISHER'S SEARCH BEGINS

In the 1960s, interest in the two galleons was renewed. Treasure hunters heard about old Spanish documents that detailed the fleet's tragic voyage. Divers began searching the shallow waters off the mid-Florida Keys, but the *Atocha* and the *Santa Margarita* remained hidden. The two elusive ships became known as the Ghost Galleons of 1622.

Searching for sunken ships and their treasures had by this time become an organized effort. It's not an easy way to get rich. It's often a matter of luck whether or not a sunken ship is discovered. Treasure hunters must raise a lot of money to pay for divers and expensive equipment. They must be adventurous, optimistic, resourceful, patient, secretive, and determined. Mel Fisher was just such a person.

Fisher joined the search for the Ghost Galleons in the Florida Keys in the late 1960s. Like others who had looked for the ships, he relied on mistaken accounts of where the ships went down. Then, in 1970, Fisher got an important break. Dr. Eugene Lyon, a researcher and friend of Fisher's, made an important discovery. Old Spanish documents that Lyon translated proved that the *Atocha* sank in a different area of the Keys, some 100 miles (161 km) away from where everyone had been looking. Fisher and his company, Treasure Salvors, relocated to Key West. They began searching near the western islands called the Marquesas (mar-KAY-sahs) Keys.

The following year Fisher's divers found the first promising object: a galleon anchor. Then an 8.5-foot-long (2.6-m) gold chain was recovered. Soon they were bringing up artifacts—objects made long ago—like barrel hoops, cannonballs, and muskets. Excitement grew when two gold bars were found. Fisher believed they were hot on the trail of the *Atocha*. Then suddenly the trail turned ice cold.

Divers found nothing over the next two years. Still, Fisher remained optimistic. Underwater searches were made easier with modern equipment and technology. His salvage ships towed a magnetometer—an instrument used like an underwater metal detector. With a friend's help, Fisher invented a device called a mailbox— an L-shaped tube that fits over a boat's propeller. While the boat is anchored, with engines running, the propellers whirl, and the tube forces water down toward the sea bottom. Blasts of water blow craters in the sand, uncovering heavy objects underneath. For more delicate work, a diver uses an airlift, which works like an underwater vacuum cleaner by sucking in sand and stones and then dumping them out through a tube.

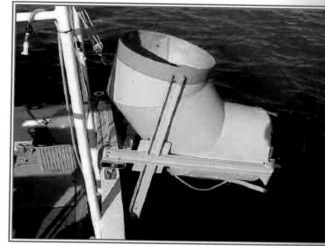

Mailbox device

GETTING CLOSE TO THE MOTHER LODE

Spirits rose in the summer of 1973 when a silver bar was located. Its serial numbers matched those of a bar listed on the *Atocha*'s cargo manifest, or list of goods. Before the year was over, Fisher's teams had found several thousand silver coins, a long gold bar, muskets, swords, daggers, scissors, a lock and key, and an astrolabe (an ancient instrument used for navigation).

An archaeologist was hired to keep track of where each item was found and to care for the valuable objects. Gold is unaffected by salt water, but other metals, like silver, develop crusts of coral and mineral deposits. Silver coins stick together in clumps. Each item needed to be cleaned, cataloged, preserved, and studied.

It appeared that they were near the mother lode—the main part of the sunken ship and its treasure—but they were wrong. The *Atocha* had only teased them. Another long stretch went by with few findings. Still, Fisher encouraged the crew each morning by saying, "Today's the day!" Everyone tried to believe him.

In 1975, Fisher's oldest son, Dirk, seemed to make a breakthrough when he located nine bronze cannons from the *Atocha*. Then tragedy struck. On July 20, Dirk, his wife, and another diver drowned when, during the night, their boat capsized and quickly sank. The accident was a devastating loss.

Eventually, the crews resumed the search, but they made very few discoveries. Year after year they battled bad weather and choppy seas and endured the scorching sun. They spent hours under water, sifting sand and finding nothing. Expenses grew. Where was the main part of the *Atocha*? Baffled, Fisher decided to turn his attention to the *Santa Margarita*. Much of this ship's treasure had been salvaged right after the initial sinking, but Fisher knew some had been left behind. The remains of the *Santa Margarita* treasure ended up being relatively easy to locate. In 1980, Fisher's team brought up enough to keep them in business.

But the whereabouts of the *Atocha* still haunted Fisher. Many times he had felt so close. . .then, nothing. He had his crews return to the search, and in the spring of 1985, they were finally rewarded. Divers recovered 13 gold bars and some emerald jewelry—and that was only the beginning. Kane Fisher, another of Fisher's sons, was about to make the discovery of a lifetime.

THE *ATOCHA* IS FOUND!

Kane Fisher was looking in an area of the ocean near where Dirk had discovered the bronze cannons ten years earlier. On July 20, 1985, exactly ten years after Dirk's death, Kane radioed his home office, "Put away the charts!

We've found the main pile!" Kane and his crew had
located the *Atocha*'s mother lode.

At first, the divers had seen what they
thought was a large pile of rubble on the sea floor.
It was 30 feet long, 20 feet wide, and 5 feet high
(9.1 x 6.1 x 1.5 m). Then they spotted large timbers
under heaps of silver bars and coins. The pile of
silver had shielded the wooden hull of the ship and
had prevented many of the timbers from rotting
away. Thrilled, the divers realized that the bulk of
the treasure had to be under this pile. The
submerged wreckage was just southwest of the
Marquesas Keys—less than 40 miles (64 km) from
Florida's Key West. The *Atocha* had been sitting
under a mere 55 feet (16.8 m) of water for 363 years.

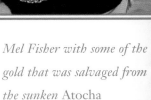

*Mel Fisher with some of the
gold that was salvaged from
the sunken* Atocha

Fisher's 16-year search had cost $8 million.
Some of the money came from profits made from his
earlier salvages, while the rest was raised through hundreds of
investors. The treasure was recovered piece by piece, and the
results were spectacular. Divers found 115 gold bars, about 32 tons
(29 metric tons) of silver, 78 gold chains, more than 3,000 emeralds,
thousands of silver coins, jewelry, and nearly 15 tons (13.6 metric tons) of
copper bars. They also retrieved artifacts with great historical value, such as
candlesticks, cups, pottery, and more.

How much was the treasure worth? Estimates have ranged between $200
and $400 million in today's money. But the *Atocha* has yet to reveal all of its
secrets. An important part of the ship remains hidden—the sterncastle, which
is the rear section where the captain and wealthy passengers stayed. The sterncastle probably contains the valuable possessions of these people, as well as
items that were being concealed in order to avoid paying taxes.

These coins and gold bars were part of the Atocha's *mother lode.*

Divers are still recovering the *Atocha*'s treasure. Some of it is scattered as far as 5 miles (8 km) from the mother lode. One theory is that after the ship sank, a later hurricane moved the stern across the ocean floor. Sadly, Fisher was able to enjoy his discovery for only 13 years. He died in 1998 at the age of 76. Before his death, however, Fisher established a museum in Key West to display some of the artifacts and treasure. Today the public can view these priceless objects and learn more about the fatal voyage of the Ghost Galleons. Mel's family and friends continue his work and plan new expeditions.

Some people dream of instant wealth. The idea that shipwrecks litter the ocean floor, and are loaded with treasures just waiting to be discovered, is irresistible. Mel Fisher proved that these dreams can come true, though not without sacrifice.

Chapter FOUR

Most divers don't worry about encountering massive sea monsters while underwater, but maybe they should. There is one "monster" that might very well lurk near sunken ships in the deepest parts of the sea. . . .

CHAPTER FIVE
Sea Monster: The Giant Squid

The monsters in movies and fairy tales are almost always big, ugly, and scary. But what about real-life monsters? Do such things actually exist? Meet the deep-sea-dwelling giant squid. Most "real" monsters have eventually been revealed as hoaxes, but not the giant squid. This monster has proven all too real.

A thousand years ago, during the Middle Ages, maps were often drawn with pictures of sea monsters bobbing in the ocean. Sailors from Norway told chilling tales of the kraken (KRAK-in), an evil monster with many long arms. Out of nowhere the kraken attacked ships, wrapping its gigantic tentacles around the vessels and pulling them under water, where the monster would then eat the helpless sailors.

A sea monster was drawn in the ocean on this map of Virginia and the Atlantic Ocean from the sixteenth century.

Could the kraken have been a giant squid? Has a giant squid ever really sunk a ship or eaten people? Let's take a look—from a safe distance—at this mysterious creature, which lurks far below the surface in the ocean's depths.

CHARACTERISTICS OF THE GIANT SQUID

The giant squid has an oddly put together body. Eight arms dangle from one end, and a pointy tail with triangular fins used for steering swings from the other. The torpedo-shaped body has a loose covering called the mantle. The head is located at the opposite end from the tail, and two lidless eyes, as big as basketballs, stare out from the sides of the head.

The squid's eight snakelike arms sprout from its head. The undersides of its thick arms are lined with rows of round suction cups called suckers. The outer rims of the suckers have sawtooth edges. These "teeth" can cut through flesh for a firmer grip. Two thin tentacles, longer than the arms, also grow from the head. Each tentacle ends in a flattened palm-shape with more suckers on it. The animal looks like an alien from another world, and in some ways it is.

The giant squid often floats motionless deep below the ocean's surface in water that's pitch black because the sun's rays don't penetrate that far down. Its huge eyes are able to pick up the movement of a big fish even in this dark water. With a whiplike motion, the tentacles grab the fish and pull it close. The eight arms help the tentacles tighten their hold. Then something shocking is revealed. In the middle of the head, encircled by the arms and tentacles, is a sharp beak. The curved, parrotlike beak tears into the fish and devours it hungrily.

Suddenly the squid is gone. Like a jet it simply swooshes away. How? Beneath the giant squid's head is a funnel, or tube, that can turn in any direction. The squid sucks water in through gills located under the mantle, and then shoots the water out of the funnel, propelling itself through the water like an underwater drag racer.

This is how scientists *think* the giant squid behaves. Not much is known about this elusive creature, because a healthy, living giant squid has never been caught. And no one has closely observed the animal in its own realm—the dark ocean depths. Specimens that have been examined were dead, or dying.

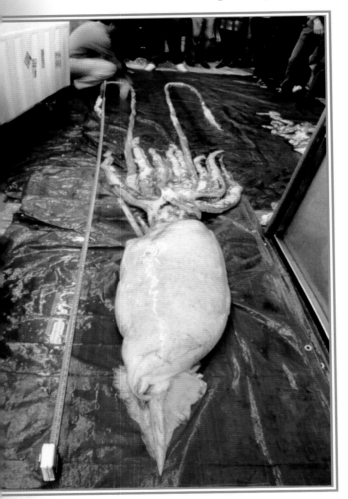

Decaying squid bodies have washed ashore onto beaches, and other squid have died after getting caught in fishing nets. Scientists have eagerly studied whatever bodies, or pieces of bodies, have been found by beachcombers and fishermen.

The largest giant squid ever found (dead) was about as long as two school buses. From its pointy tail to the ends of its long tentacles, it stretched nearly 60 feet (18.3 m), and weighed about 2,000 pounds (907 kg). Some researchers believe that even larger squid measuring up to 100 feet long (30.5 m) might dwell in the deep waters. We just don't know for sure.

RUN-INS WITH SEA MONSTERS

Back in the 1800s, crews on whaling ships would notice big undigested squid beaks in the stomachs of dead sperm whales. Occasionally, before dying, a sperm whale would vomit up chunks of squid bodies, arms, and tentacles, all of which hinted at the squid's great size. Then, in 1861, a living giant squid was spotted at sea for the first time. Near the Canary Islands, off the northwest coast of Africa in the Atlantic Ocean, a lookout

This dead giant squid was netted off the coast of New Zealand in 1997. It measured 25 feet (7.6 m) long and weighted 250 pounds (113.4 kg).

on a French warship spied an enormous dark-red-bodied beast near the surface. Shipmates stared into the "large glimmering eyes of the monster." It was estimated to be 18 feet (5.5 m) long, not counting its tentacles.

Frightened sailors fired shots at the monster, causing it to dive. When the beast reappeared, a noose was thrown around it. But the rope cut right through the body, and the head, arms, and tentacles fell back into the water. Only the tail section was hauled on board. A squid's blood is clear blue, not red, and the sailors shuddered at the blue blood streaming from the creature's body. The ship's commanding officer filed a detailed report. Describing the monster's mouth, he wrote, ". . .its large mouth, shaped like the beak of a parakeet, could open nearly a half meter." That's about 20 inches. A mouth that size could deliver a massive bite.

Scientists who have studied the report are certain that this "monster" was actually a giant squid. The floating animal was probably already dying before its encounter with the ship, because it's now known that healthy giant squid remain between 600 and 3,200 feet (183–975 m) below the surface.

Old drawing of some sailors trying to catch a giant squid

On rare occasions, however, a giant squid has been seen at the ocean's surface, battling its number one enemy, the sperm whale. The sperm whale is the only animal known to dive to the depths of the ocean in order to retrieve a giant squid supper. Witnesses have told of vicious combat between the two giants. Picture the sight: a 60-foot (18.3-m) sperm whale breaks the surface of the ocean with its head wrapped in giant squid tentacles. The whale triumphs after a ferocious fight. But it probably bears marks from the squid's suckers and gashes from the sharp beak.

Could it be that ancient legends about sea serpents originated in scenes like this? Imagine how terrifying it would have been to see these massive tentacles coiled around a sperm whale. It's easy to understand how sailors witnessing such events hundreds of years ago might begin telling tales of giant sea serpents.

WHAT DO WE KNOW ABOUT THE GIANT SQUID?

We know that like all squids, the giant squid belongs to the mollusk group, which is made up of animals with soft, boneless bodies. Snails, slugs, and octopuses are also mollusks. Squids and octopuses are a part of the mollusk group called cephalopods (SEF-uh-luh-podz), which means "feet in the head" in Greek.

Here's what else we know:

◆ It likely can change the color of its skin from a pale gray to a speckled dark red.

◆ Inside its body is an ink sac. When threatened, the squid squirts dark ink, which makes it hard for its enemy to see it.

◆ The giant squid can stay afloat without swimming.

◆ Its muscle tissues contain an ammonium solution that it can adjust to make itself lighter or heavier. This gives its flesh a bitter ammonia taste. Sperm whales don't seem to mind, but it should prevent the giant squid from ever becoming a popular menu item.

Chapter FIVE

WHAT DON'T WE KNOW ABOUT THE GIANT SQUID?

Here are a few questions we have about this animal:

◆ How long does it live?

◆ How big can it grow?

◆ How does it hunt and catch prey?

◆ How does it reproduce?

◆ Are adults rare, or do they exist in large numbers?

◆ Do they live in groups?

◆ Do they have enemies other than sperm whales?

The most puzzling question is how an animal this large has remained out of sight for so long. The brain of a giant squid is big, which means the squid is probably intelligent. This could explain how and why it avoids us. To get an idea of just how smart the giant squid might be, we can look at the octopus. Because octopuses and squid are closely related and because both have large brains, scientists think their intelligence levels are probably similar. And we know that octopuses are quite smart. In one experiment two octopuses were kept in adjoining glass water tanks. Researchers put a group of balls into one of the tanks. There were red balls and white ones, and the octopus was taught that by selecting a red ball, it could get a treat. It took only a short time to teach the octopus which ball to choose, based on the ball's color.

That's pretty amazing, but here is the really impressive part. When the same balls were put into the adjoining tank with the second octopus, no lessons were needed. This octopus picked the correct ball. It had learned what it needed to do to get a treat just by watching the other octopus! The giant squid is probably equally smart.

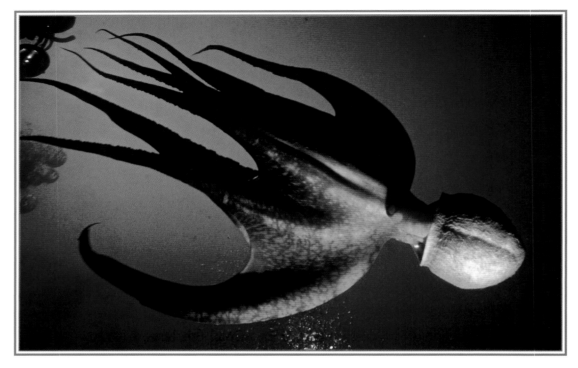

Octopuses, like this giant Pacific octopus (above), and squid, like this jumbo squid (below), are closely related and look alike.

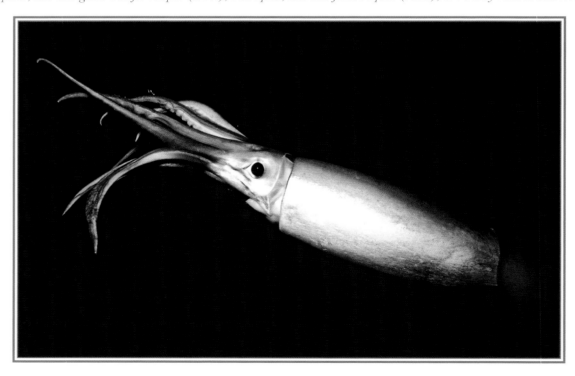

Chapter FIVE

HUMAN PREDATOR?

From the stomach contents of dead giant squid, scientists have learned that this animal eats fish, octopuses, and even other squid. But has a giant squid ever attacked ships or eaten humans? Over the years fishermen in small boats have encountered the huge animal, and their stories are usually similar. Something is spotted floating in the water. Upon closer examination the "thing" suddenly "opens like an umbrella." Large dark eyes stare at the surprised onlookers. Then, thrashing tentacles and arms grab the boat. In many cases the men have to chop off a tentacle or arm before the creature releases the boat. The shaken fishermen then watch as the strange animal disappears in a pool of dark ink.

Small boats have been attacked, but what about people being eaten? In 1874, an incident was reported in the London *Times*. A ship carrying eight men was becalmed and drifting when, as the captain later said, "a great mass rose slowly out of the sea." As the squid came toward the ship, the captain fired at it with a rifle. The creature kept coming. With its long arms, it heaved itself onto the ship. The panicky crew slashed the squid with axes. As the animal fell back into the water, its flailing arms grasped the edge of the small ship, which was pulled onto its side and began to sink. A nearby steamship hurried to the rescue. Seven of the men on the schooner survived, but one man was never found. No one knew whether he drowned or became the squid's lunch.

Books and movies alike portray the giant squid as an aggressive people-killer, but in reality, this animal seems to avoid people as much as possible. No proof exists that a giant squid has ever actually eaten a person. However, as long as so much remains a mystery about this largest of the cephalopods, some people will continue to view it as a scary monster.

Will a living, healthy giant squid ever be found? In September 2005, there was an exciting breakthrough: For the first time ever, a giant squid was photographed in its natural habitat deep below the ocean's surface. A Japanese

A giant squidlike monster attacks a boat in this six-teenth century engraving.

research team reported that they had encountered a 26-foot-long (8-m) giant squid a year earlier. In the fall of 2004, they lowered a shrimp-baited rope down to 3,000 feet (914.4 m) below the surface, and a robotic camera snapped hundreds of photos, including the ones of the giant squid. When the researchers retrieved the rope, an 18-foot-long (5.5-m) tentacle was stuck to it. The squid wouldn't grow another tentacle, but it could live with just one.

Although the photographs provided new information about this elusive animal's behavior, biologists still hope to someday safely capture a giant squid to examine more closely. In the meantime, researchers will continue their search using submersibles and robotic cameras.

The average depth of Earth's oceans is about 12,000 feet (3,658 m), plunging as deep as 36,000 feet—almost 7 miles (11 km)—in some areas. We know more about the moon than we do about the ocean floor. Scientists have explored only about 5 percent of Earth's vast waters. That leaves plenty of territory in which the giant squid can roam.

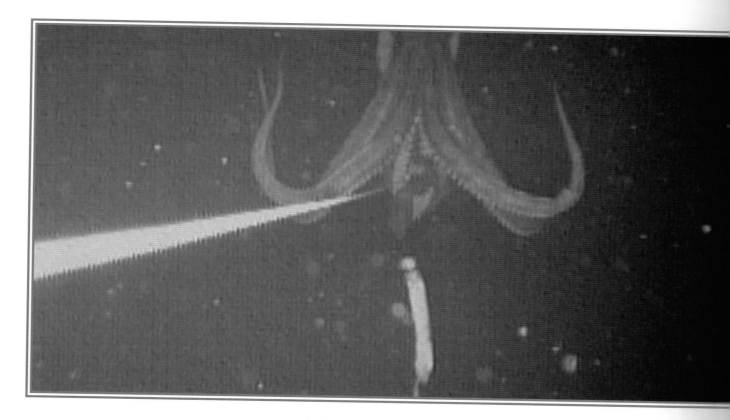

Far away from the giant squid's habitat, a revolting creature swims in lakes and streams. It's only an inch or so in length, but many people react to this animal as if it were a monster. Can you guess what it is?

In October 2004, Japanese scientists took this photo that, for the first time, shows a live giant squid in its natural habitat, but they didn't release the photo until September 2005. The squid, which was purplish red, is shown attacking bait hung from a white rope.

CHAPTER SIX
∾ The Blood-Sucking Leech

Many people have just one word to say about the slimy, wormlike leech: "Yuck!" In a famous old movie scene, a shirtless man wades slowly through chest-high water, straining to pull his small boat through an African marsh. When he struggles back into the boat, his female companion shrieks in horror. The man's bare chest and back are studded with dozens of 2-inch-long (5.1-cm) black leeches. Their mouths cling to the man's skin, greedily sucking his blood.

During this vivid scene, viewers shuddered in disgust, and the leech's reputation as a repulsive parasite was sealed. A parasite is any animal or plant that lives off of another organism. But despite this, the vampire-like leech isn't all bad. Would you believe that some people even pay to have these bloodthirsty critters attached to their skin? It's true. These often misunderstood creatures have a helpful side.

LEECH CHARACTERISTICS

The leech is part of the worm family. There are several hundred species of leeches, ranging in size from about the length of your smallest fingernail up to whoppers that stretch 18 or more inches (45.7 cm) long. Their bodies are flatter than most other worms, and when resting, they shrink into an oval leaflike shape.

Leeches can be black, brown, or red, and a few even have spots or stripes. This animal's only eyes are light-sensitive cells located near its front end. It has

∾

a disk-like sucker at each end of its body; in the front sucker is a mouth with three jaws full of tiny teeth.

Where are leeches found? Rather, where are you likely to be when leeches find you? Most leech species live in streams or lakes. When a leech latches on to you, it sticks to your skin with its posterior (rear) sucker. Then the front sucker-mouth attaches, the three jaws carve a shallow Y-shaped wound, and the worm begins to suck your blood. Leech saliva has a natural painkiller, so most people don't feel a thing. The saliva

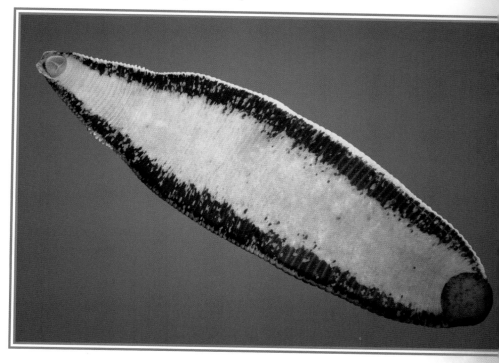

also contains a chemical that prevents blood from clotting, called *The underside of a leech at rest* hirudin (hir-YOOD-in), which makes it easier for the worm to drain your blood.

After the parasite finishes gorging, it falls off. Many leeches can hold between five and ten times their own weight in blood. When full, a leech looks like a fat cigar—not a pretty sight. A blood-filled leech can go about six months between feedings.

Not all leeches are bloodsucking parasites. Some are scavengers that live off dead and decayed animal or plant material. Other species nibble soft-bodied critters such as slugs and snails. Instead of jaws, some leeches have a needlelike snout, or proboscis (pro-BOHS-is), that they insert into their prey like a straw and use to slurp up soft body tissue or blood.

A leech is an invertebrate, meaning it has no backbone. Its closest relative is the earthworm. Both leeches and earthworms are annelids (AN-uh-lidz)—worms with segmented bodies. Species of leeches are able to survive in places as different as alpine mountains and polar oceans. Land leeches prefer warm, wet climates. They walk with a looping movement, similar to an inchworm. The most common leeches, however, are the freshwater ones that live in streams and lakes. When swimming, their bodies flatten and then they move through the water with an up-and-down motion. These bloodsucking leeches get their meals from fish, frogs, turtles—and an occasional human.

Leech attached to a man's arm

If you find a leech stuck to your skin after a dip in a lake or stream, don't panic. Most of the time the worms are merely annoying. Sprinkling salt or vinegar on a leech will cause it to drop off—with a minimum amount of grossness. Some people, though, have had horrible leech experiences. During wartime, thirsty soldiers crossing the Sinai Peninsula in Egypt drank from waterholes that, unknown to them, were infested with tiny leeches. The leeches attached to the insides of the men's throats, began sucking their blood, and grew larger and larger, blocking the men's air passages. The doomed victims slowly suffocated.

Chapter SIX

LEECHES USED IN MEDICINE

Yes, some leeches can be scary and disgusting. But what about the helpful, medicinal leech? This leech has a long history of treating humans. Hundreds of years ago, doctors believed that certain illnesses could be cured by draining what they called a patient's "bad blood." Called bloodletting, it was a common practice— even George Washington reportedly had it done. However, in many cases, rather than curing a person, the bloodletting caused patients to grow weaker from the loss of blood.

So where is the leech's value? The medical world has discovered that the leech can indeed be helpful in certain situations. For example, surgeons sometimes use medicinal leeches when reattaching severed body parts, such as fingers or ears. In 1985, a young boy's ear was bitten off by a dog. When the surgeon reattached the ear, dangerous blood clots formed. Medication to keep his blood from clotting did not help. The desperate surgeon decided to apply two medicinal leeches to the areas containing the blood clots. Slowly the creatures filled with blood, dropping off when they were full. Doctors applied several more leeches to the boy's ear over the following week. Eventually, the ear was saved. How did the leeches help?

If the blood in a person's thumb is clotting, a doctor might put a medicinal leech on the thumb, which can stop the blood from clotting and allow the thumb to heal.

We know that leech saliva has a painkilling chemical

and one that keeps blood from clotting, but added to this mix is an ingredient that keeps blood vessels open. This is why blood can trickle from a wound for more than 30 minutes after a leech falls off—the blood doesn't clot, and the blood vessels stay open. Free-flowing blood is important after surgeons reattach a severed body part, because good circulation leads to healing. The leeches on the boy's ear got rid of the blood clots and allowed his blood to circulate, enabling the wound to heal properly. Scientists also believe that leech saliva can prevent bacteria from infecting a wound. It's powerful stuff!

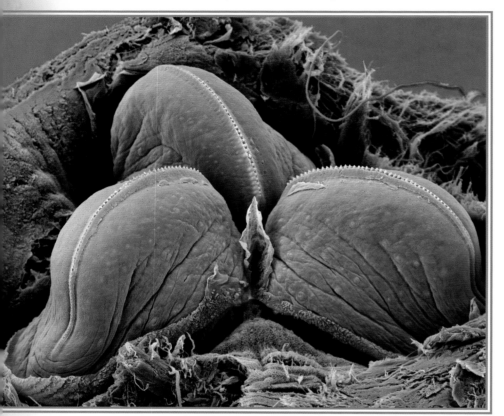

This close up of a medicinal leech's mouth shows the three jaws that leave a Y-shaped wound.

Because of the medicinal benefit of some leeches, leech farms have sprung up where some species of leeches are raised in special tanks. The creatures then are shipped to hospitals and research labs around the world, and scientists study the leeches and their remarkable saliva. Recent discoveries point to future treatments for cancer, heart attacks, and strokes. Studies of the leech's nervous system reveal more about how nerve cells work in general, which could lead to new information about human learning problems and birth defects. The medical field is so confident about the leech's importance to medicine that, in the summer of 2004, the United States

Food and Drug Administration (FDA) approved the use of the leech as a medical device.

Most people agree that the lowly leech does not have lovable looks or feeding habits. Leeches are usually described as slimy, ugly, or disgusting. However, this amazing invertebrate offers exciting possibilities for improving our lives. Who knows, perhaps someday we'll celebrate "Love-a-Leech Day!" Stranger things have happened.

An animal much larger than a leech dwells in a deep Scottish lake. Or is it just a legend? Myths and legends sometimes sprout from grains of truth. This monster legend has stuck around for centuries. Read on to discover what it is.

7

CHAPTER SEVEN

Is the Loch Ness Monster Real?

You've been sitting by the lake in the chilly air for hours. Next to you a camera is perched on a tripod. The light breeze becomes a steady wind that ruffles the lake's surface. Shivering, you gaze across the wide body of murky water. You notice movement at the water's surface. You squint and try to make out what's out there. Wide-eyed with shock, you watch as a long, thin neck rises out of the water. At the end of the neck, a snakelike head slowly turns as the beast looks around. Its broad back resembles an upside-down boat. Seconds later the creature dives back under the surface. The dark gray creature is gone. Only the expanding ripples mark the place from which it emerged.

Heart pounding, you remain frozen to the spot. That's when you realize you didn't take a picture. But you saw it! The strange beast was there in the water. Will anyone believe that you glimpsed the Loch Ness Monster? They'll insist that what you saw must've been a log or a floating bird or a big wave. But you know better. It was alive, enormous, and it looked similar to what others have described.

THE LEGEND OF LOCH NESS

Curious people have been coming to scenic northern Scotland to visit Loch Ness, near the town of Inverness, for years. The loch (the Scottish word for *lake*) empties into the River Ness, which flows for 7 miles (11.3 km) before spilling into the North Sea. Loch Ness is huge: 23 miles long, a mile wide

Loch Ness in Scotland. Castle Urquhart (ER-kart), which was built in the thirteenth century, is visible on the lake's edge.

(37 x 1.6 km), and nearly 800 feet (273.8 m) deep in some places.

Loch Ness was once a part of the North Sea, but about 12,000 years ago, the Ice Age changed the landscape. The loch was mostly cut off from the sea, connected only by the River Ness at the loch's northern end. Massive slow-moving ice chiseled the lake's steep rocky sides and carved ledges and caves into the underwater rock.

Loch Ness is fed by mountain streams that flow through highland bogs and then dump mossy plant matter into the lake. The peat-filled water is dark brown. Divers find it impossible to see more than a few feet through the watery gloom. The loch never gets cold enough to freeze, but the surface water temperature averages a chilly 58 degrees Fahrenheit (14.4° C). At the lake's bottom, the temperature falls to 42 degrees Fahrenheit (5.6° C).

The Scottish lake is the perfect setting for a mystery. Hazy mists sometimes hover over it. Shadowy ruins of a thirteenth century castle stand like a ghostly protector on a bluff overlooking the waters. On both sides of the length of the lake, hilly land turns into mountains shaded by trees and shrubs.

The legend of the Loch Ness Monster is over 1,000 years old. The first recorded sighting was in A.D. 565. As the story goes, a man was crossing Loch Ness when a water monster lunged at him. From the nearby shore, a Christian priest, later known as Saint Columba, glared at the beast and shouted, "Stop! Go thou no further nor touch the man." Immediately the monster disappeared into the water. Saint Columba had saved the man's life.

Thousands of sightings have occurred since then, mostly by people in the local villages who shared tales of the "great beastie." Eventually, however, the outside world heard about the monster, too. In 1933, construction workers widened a road that ran next to Loch Ness. For the first time, travelers on the road could see a 20-mile (32.2-km) portion of the lake. One day a couple named Mr. and Mrs. Mackay were driving along the lake. Mrs. Mackay gasped as she saw "an enormous body" rise out of the water. Her husband slammed on the brakes to stop the car. The astonished couple watched the huge beast thrash in the churning water. Suddenly it plunged beneath the waves and did not reappear. A local newspaper reported the event in dramatic detail, and other papers soon picked up and printed the fascinating story.

WHAT IS NESSIE SUPPOSED TO LOOK LIKE?

More sightings followed, leading to greater publicity. People wondered if the road construction's blasting had stirred the mysterious aquatic animal, now nicknamed "Nessie." Witnesses generally describe Nessie as having the following characteristics:

This photo of the Loch Ness Monster from 1934 was later proved to be a hoax.

- ◆ a heavy body of dark brown or gray
- ◆ a length ranging from about 15 to 50 feet (4.6–15.2 m)
- ◆ a back with a ridge, like an upturned boat, or a back with one to three humps
- ◆ a long tapered tail
- ◆ a long slim neck
- ◆ a snakelike head, often with two stumpy horns

Nessie stuffed animals for sale in Scotland

◆ two to four diamond-shaped fins or flippers

◆ no aggression toward humans—Nessie is shy

In recent years the Loch Ness Monster has been pictured in cartoon drawings as a friendly looking dinosaur. Can this creature be taken seriously? Is there any truth to the legend?

THE BELIEVERS VS. THE SKEPTICS

Since the 1960s, scientists have been examining the loch's cold, murky water using fancy equipment like small subs, computer scanners, underwater

Chapter SEVEN

What Nonbelievers Say	What Believers Say
There is no physical evidence that Nessie exists—not even a skin sample or a tooth.	Physical evidence, like skin or a tooth, is difficult to find. The thick peat and lack of plants in the loch cause the water to be acidic and low in oxygen. This causes objects such teeth, scales, or skin to sink to the bottom.
Photographs and videotapes are always fuzzy or too far away to prove anything. Many are obvious fakes, and all others are controversial.	It's agreed that some of the Nessie sightings and photos are hoaxes, while others are honest mistakes. However, many of the reports cannot be so easily rejected. The water's murkiness makes clear underwater pictures impossible, but some computer-enhanced images have shown an outline of a bulky body with a long neck. Another has shown a flipper-like object, and a third image appears to be a close-up of Nessie's head. (Skeptics argue that these images are actually just tree stumps or underwater debris.)
Nessie is great for tourism. Nessie-seekers buy souvenirs and fill hotels and restaurants. No wonder Scottish people keep the legend alive.	With thousands of sightings over the years, Nessie must be taken seriously. Many reliable witnesses are from outside the area and aren't trying to boost tourism.
Researchers have found no proof of a Loch Ness Monster. For example in 1987, Operation Deep Scan was conducted. A line of 19 boats with sonar moved across the lake. The entire lake was searched, but no monster was found.	Nothing definite was found during the 1987 Operation Deep Scan project, but the sonar did reveal some large unidentified shapes. Ten years later, in 1997, a boat crew using sonar tracked 15-foot-long (4.5-m) creatures moving deep beneath the surface. (Skeptics claim that these could be schools of fish.)
The lake's food supply is poor. Light cannot get through the peat-filled water, so plants do not grow under water. With such a small amount of plant life in Loch Ness, there's not enough food to support large beasts.	The lack of plants in the loch wouldn't matter if Nessie were a fish-eater. Both salmon and small eels migrate to Loch Ness from the North Sea. Some witnesses describe panicky fish leaping up from the water. The fish dart away from something chasing them. From the size of the surging waves, the underwater "something" must be huge.
No animal exists that looks like the creature people claim to have seen. The closest specimen was a plesiosaur (PLEE-see-uh-sor), an extinct reptile that lived 70 million years ago. But no reptile could survive in the loch because it's too cold. Also, reptiles breathe air, but Nessie doesn't seem to surface often enough to get the air she'd need to survive.	Nessie might be related to, but different from, plesiosaurs. Perhaps it's an amphibian that adapted to the fresh water of the loch after the Ice Age. Biologists discover new species of animals all the time. Occasionally, species thought to be extinct reappear.

Another supposed photo of the Loch Ness Monster that was later revealed as a fake

strobe lights hooked up to cameras, and sonar. With sonar, researchers can measure the size, distance, and movement of any object in the loch. No solid proof of Nessie's existence has been uncovered. So why doesn't this monster story go away? Believers and nonbelievers debate the possibility of a Loch Ness Monster.

Some people are not convinced by these believers' theories. Critics insist that the Loch Ness Monster is just a modern version of an ancient Scottish myth about kelpies (KEL-peez). In Scottish mythology a kelpie is a horselike water fairy that entices people to take a ride, but then when the person mounts the kelpie, he or she becomes stuck to the kelpie's back. Then when the kelpie jumps into the water, the helpless rider drowns.

Chapter SEVEN

Could this be the origin of the Loch Ness Monster, or is it a real living animal? One thing is for sure: The hunt for the elusive creature will continue despite the doubters. The believers will keep searching. On shore, amateurs will peer through binoculars, hoping to see Nessie, and scientists armed with the latest equipment will examine the depths of Loch Ness again and again, hoping to find proof that the mysterious monster truly exists.

While Nessie remains a mystery, the next water wonder is most definitely real. It's also huge and loud, and its admirers range from daredevils to poets. What might it be?

CHAPTER EIGHT
‿ Niagara Falls: Natural Wonder

On an October day in 1901, eager spectators lined the shores of the Niagara River on the border of Ontario, Canada, and New York State. They watched as Annie Taylor squeezed into a 4-1/2-foot (1.4-m)-high oak barrel and buckled herself into a special harness. An assistant tapped the heavy lid into place, and the barrel was lowered into the river with Annie in it. Two men in a small boat towed the barrel toward the Canadian side of the river. One of the men unfastened the towrope, and the barrel started downriver, bobbing and spinning and then picking up speed as it entered the rapids. Annie's barrel was racing toward the towering Niagara Falls.

Annie Taylor, a 63-year-old former schoolteacher from Michigan, was not a typical daredevil. But she was determined to be the first person to plunge over the Niagara Falls in a barrel—and to survive the stunt. Two cushions and a pillow padded the inside of her cramped container. A heavy iron block in the barrel's base kept it upright.

It took about 18 minutes for Annie's barrel to reach the edge of the nearly 180-foot (55-m) falls. The breathtaking drop took only

Annie Taylor being helped out of the water after her trip over the falls in a barrel

‿

seconds. Upon hitting the water at the base of the falls, the barrel sank below the surface. It shot up out of the water and into the air, fell again, and then disappeared.

Annie later said, "I felt myself whirled about and lifted like butter in a churn." Soon she felt the wood scrape the riverbed. Men waiting on a big rock nearby grabbed the rope attached to the barrel and pulled it ashore. One of the men pried off the lid and peeked in. "The woman is alive!" he shouted. The crowd cheered as Annie emerged from the barrel, bruised and bleeding from a gash on her head. She was shaken, but hadn't broken any bones. Annie Taylor declared that she would never do that again and warned others not to attempt it either.

However, in the 100 plus years since Annie's trip down the falls, many others have attempted the death-defying feat. Some rode in barrels, while others carried out the stunt in contraptions made from canvas inner tubes, plastic, steel, and more. Not everyone succeeded. The raging falls claimed several lives.

Historical illustration of a man who has just traveled over the falls in a barrel

HOW BIG ARE THE NIAGARA FALLS?

Most people don't visit Niagara Falls to see dangerous stunts, however. Each year millions of visitors go to witness the falls' spectacular beauty. Painters, photographers, writers, and poets have tried to capture the majesty of the falling waters many times. Rising from the base of the falls, a rainbow glows softly in clouds of mist. At night tourists gasp in wonder as beams of multicolored lights illuminate the waters. Considered a romantic getaway, Niagara has long been a popular destination for honeymooners.

Water Wonders of the World

As waterfalls go, Niagara doesn't rank among the tallest. The falls are only about as tall as a 16-story building. California alone has several waterfalls that are taller. But many of the higher waterfalls are narrow trickles. In contrast, the wide expanse of Niagara Falls sends 748,000 gallons (2,832 kl) of water spilling over their crests each second.

Niagara Falls, showing both the American and Horseshoe Falls, and Goat Island between them

Niagara Falls is actually made up of two separate waterfalls: the American Falls (in New York) and the Horseshoe Falls (in Canada). A small island called Goat Island separates the two falls. The American Falls, at 1,060 feet (323.1 m) wide, are overshadowed by the impressive Horseshoe Falls, which stretch 2,600 feet (792.5 m) across—almost half a mile wide! The falls' great expanse is what makes them so spectacular.

Between Goat Island (yes, goats once grazed there) and the New York shore lies tiny Luna Island. This island diverts some of the American Falls' water to a separate cascade (kas-KAYD), the picturesque Luna Falls—which are often called the Bridal Veil Falls. A cascade is a small waterfall; a large waterfall is a cataract (KAT-uh-rakt).

Chapter EIGHT

HOW WERE THE NIAGARA FALLS FORMED?

Many of the world's waterfalls were formed over two million years ago. Niagara Falls, however, are comparatively young—they were formed only about 12,000 years ago. During the last Ice Age, huge glaciers covered much of North America. Grinding movements of the glaciers carved out large chunks of earth under the thick ice. As the earth grew warmer, water from melting glaciers filled the glacier-made hollows. Thousands of lakes and rivers were created, including the Great Lakes (Michigan, Superior, Huron, Erie, and Ontario). These five bodies of water are the largest group of fresh water lakes in the world.

The upper lakes (Michigan, Superior, and Huron) drained into Lake Erie. Overflowing water from Lake Erie formed the Niagara River. This river is what fuels Niagara Falls. Beginning quietly at Lake Erie, near Buffalo, New York, the river flows slowly north. About halfway down the 35-mile-long (56.3-km) river, the shallow, rocky riverbed slopes, causing the water to pick up speed and form rapids. The water speed reaches a swift-moving 20 miles per hour (32 kph) near the crest of the falls. Here the riverbed drops away, leaving a vertical underwater cliff. This is where the dramatic plunge of tons of water happens.

After the water splashes down to the bottom of the falls, it rushes downstream to more swift currents and the dangerous Whirlpool Rapids. This deep pool of violently swirling water creates a current so fierce that it has scooped out a 125-foot-deep (38.1-m) basin out of the rock. Beyond the Whirlpool Rapids, the river grows calmer. Finally it empties into Lake Ontario.

HISTORY OF THE FALLS

For thousands of years, the only people who knew of the falls' existence were the Native Americans who lived in the area. The earliest known history of the region is from the 1500s, when the Seneca (SEN-uh-cuh) tribe controlled the Niagara area. They spoke a language called Iroquois (IHR-uh-kwah). In this

*The Whirlpool
Rapids at
Niagara Falls*

language, *Niagara* means "thunder of water." The Seneca used the Niagara River as a trade route, but because the falls and the Whirlpool Rapids made parts of the river impassable, they had to get out and walk some 9 miles (14.5 km) alongside the river. This harsh part of the journey pushed through thick brush on a path so steep that it became known as "crawl-on-all-fours" trail.

The first European to write about the falls was a Belgian priest, Louis Hennepin, who accompanied a French expedition. He viewed the falls in December 1678, and described what he saw:

. . .There is an incredible Cataract or Waterfall, which has no equal. The Niagara River near this place is only the eighth of a league* wide, but it is very deep in places, and so rapid above the great fall that it hurries down all the animals which try to cross it, without a single one being able to withstand its current. They plunge down a height of more than 500 feet, and its fall is composed of two sheets of water and a cascade, with an island sloping down. In the middle these waters foam and boil in a fearful manner.

* One league equals about 3 miles (4.8 km), so an eighth of a league is about 1,980 feet (604 m).

Chapter EIGHT

Europeans reading this exaggerated description thought Niagara Falls to be more than twice their actual height. One hundred years passed before painters who visited the falls presented more accurate descriptions.

When the French explorer La Salle (luh SAL) came to the Niagara River in 1679, he constructed a fort and established a French presence. Throughout most of the late seventeenth century and much of the eighteenth century, French and British troops fought over the territory along the river. Native Americans living in the area battled soldiers of both countries but were unable to hold onto their lands.

The United States didn't lay claim to the area until 1783, after the Revolutionary War had ended. At that time they claimed the east bank of the Niagara River. The west bank eventually became part of Canada. The falls' reputation grew as awestruck visitors from Europe sent home word of the spectacular sight. Niagara Falls became one of the main symbols of the United States to foreigners and remained so until the Statue of Liberty was erected in 1886. Visitors felt their trip overseas wasn't complete without a view of the thundering waters.

Historical drawing of Father Hennepin viewing Niagara Falls in 1678

Throughout the 1800s a circus-like atmosphere surrounded the falls. Performers and daredevils used them as a backdrop for death-defying acts. People flocked to see entertainers walk on ropes or wires stretched across the river below the waterfall. The acts became more and more daring. One performer walked a tightrope while blindfolded. Another walked backwards. The next entertainer carried a person on his back, while yet another balanced a chair on the rope, sat down, and read a newspaper. Today stunts like these are illegal, and barrel riders face arrest plus a fine of at least $10,000.

EROSION AND CHANGE

At the time of their creation some 12,000 years ago, Niagara Falls stood about seven miles downstream from today's location. Erosion from the crashing waters has caused the falls to retreat as much as 6 feet (1.8 m) a year and also to grow wider. Scientists have managed to slow the pace of the erosion by rerouting some of the water before it reaches the falls. And metal rods inserted into the rocks under the Falls add strength and stability. These days the wide Horseshoe Falls move back about a foot (30.5 cm) each year, while the narrower American Falls lose only about an inch. This difference is due mostly to the amount of water pounding the rocks.

In 1969, United States Army engineers actually stopped the flow of water over the American Falls and redirected the water to the Horseshoe Falls by building a temporary dam of dirt and rock. They did this so scientists could study the layers of rock and try to figure out how to prevent future rock slides. But the experts decided that nature should be allowed to take its own course, and therefore didn't take any significant steps to prevent rock slides.

A performer walking on a tightrope over the Whirlpool Rapids in 1890

If you visit Niagara Falls today, you can put on a raincoat and take a ride on a *Maid of the Mist* boat, which cruises near the base of the falls. You'll be able to experience first-hand the incredible power and deafening roar of the water as it hurtles over the edge. You can put on another raincoat and walk along a path leading to caves behind the falls, as the water pours down in front of you. Downriver, you can take a thrilling ride in the Spanish Aero Car, a cagelike car suspended high above the rushing river. The car moves on heavy cables spanning the churning water and the dangerous Whirlpool Rapids.

Chapter EIGHT

Numerous paths, tunnels, and observation platforms offer views of the falls from many different angles. The churning cascades, cataracts, whirlpools, and rapids are incredible to behold and have a magical effect on people. The sheer beauty of Niagara Falls reminds us to appreciate the power of nature.

Maid of the Mist *tour boat in front of the Horseshoe Falls*

Leaving these awesome falling waters, we return to the sea to search for a creature that has stirred imaginations for centuries. Is it real?

9

CHAPTER NINE
❧ Mermaids: Imaginary Wonders?

A lifeless body washed up on a sandy beach. The news spread quickly throughout the island, and before long a crowd had gathered on the beach, staring and whispering. The sheriff was called in to examine the strange dead creature. What was it? The upper half of the body looked like a small woman with long dark hair. But the lower half was "like a salmon without scales."

This incident occurred in 1830 on an island off the northwest coast of Scotland. The sheriff and other witnesses became convinced that the body was part human. They covered her and then buried her in a small coffin. "She was a mermaid," the islanders agreed.

Three years later six Scottish fishermen claimed they'd caught a similar creature. Tangled in their nets, the mermaid shrieked and sobbed for hours. Her voice was humanlike. When the frazzled fishermen could no longer put up with her cries, they released her back into the sea.

Illustration of mermaids by Flora White, from the book Peter Pan *by J.M. Barrie*

What were these sea creatures? Do half-human, half-fish animals exist? Have they *ever* existed? Or are mermaids simply a part of our folklore—tales handed down from generation to

❧

generation? One thing is certain: Mermaids have been popping up in stories and artwork for centuries.

MERMAID HISTORY AND LEGEND

As early as 5,000 B.C., mermaids and mermen appeared in the art of Babylonia. (Babylonia, an ancient empire, does not exist today. It was located where Iraq is now.) Statues depict them as gods and goddesses of the waters. In ancient Greek myths, beautiful women with tails like fish were called sirens. Sirens swam near sharp, dangerous rocks, singing enchanting melodies and luring sailors who were unable to resist the music. Attracted by the hypnotic songs of the sirens, the men sailed their ships too close and crashed on the rocks, killing all on board. (The word *siren*—a high-pitched sound warning of danger—comes from the sirens of mythology.)

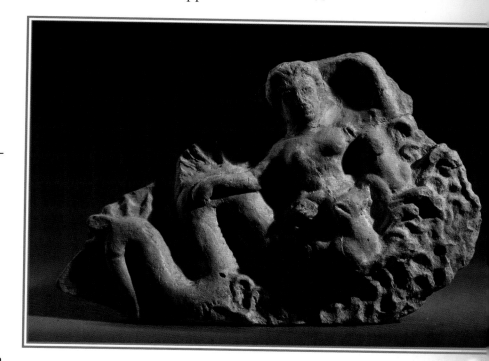

Ancient Greek sculpture of a mermaid from the late fifth century B.C.

Many cultures have legends about water maidens. These maidens are called by a variety of names—sea nymphs, water sprites, lake ladies, sea fairies, or the most familiar, mermaids—even though they have common traits. Mermaids are often portrayed as being independent and self-assured. Sometimes the mermaid punishes anyone who angers her and rewards those who help her.

In some legends a mermaid is able to breathe air for only a short time. Then she must go back underwater. In other legends she avoids direct sunlight, but on cloudy days she might sit on a rock near the shoreline. Holding a mirror, the mermaid combs her long hair. Mermaids in legends are usually beautiful, but the rare mermen are often ugly and cruel. In Scottish mythology there are stories of mermen who change into water horses and then tempt humans to ride on their backs. Once on the creature's back, however, the person is stuck and can't get off. The water horse then plunges into deep water, drowning his helpless rider.

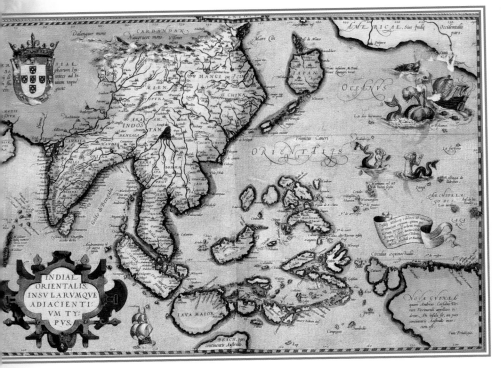

Old map with mermaids drawn in the waters

Long ago mapmakers would draw mermaids on sea charts, and artists included water maidens in their paintings of seascapes. Many people believed in mermaids, and occasional sightings kept the idea alive. One recorded sighting came during Columbus's voyage to America in 1492. According to Columbus's journal, the captain and some of his crew saw three mermaids: "They were not as beautiful as they are painted, although to some extent they have a human appearance in the face. . . ." Columbus also reported that several of his crew spotted similar-looking mermaids on an earlier voyage off the coast of West Africa.

Some seamen believed mermaids were water witches that were to blame for rough seas during storms. Superstitious sailors tossed coins into the sea, hoping to bribe the wicked mermaids into keeping the ocean calm. During storms some sailors threw daggers into the violently heaving waves in an effort to frighten the mermaids away and put an end to the rough seas.

In 1608, an English navigator named Henry Hudson recorded another mermaid sighting in his journal. Two of his crew claimed to have seen her near a group of islands off the coast of northern Russia. Hudson noted their description: "From the navel upward. . .she was like a woman. . .her body as big as one of us, her skin very white, and long hair hanging down of color black. In her going down we saw her tail, which was like the tail of a porpoise, and speckled like a mackerel."

Reports of mermaid sightings eventually led to hoaxes. Large fish were cut, shaped, and dried, and then the hoaxers gave them faces and arms so they'd look part human. More realistic fakes were created by joining parts of dead animals—for example, the upper half of a shaved monkey attached to the bottom half of a fish.

In the 1840s, the showman P. T. Barnum exhibited a famous phony mermaid in his museum. People waited in long lines to see what they believed to be a real mermaid. Barnum later described it as "ugly, dried-up and black looking." How could imitations like these fool people into paying money to view them? As Barnum reportedly said, "There's a sucker born every minute!"

Above: Historical poster of Barnum and Bailey from 1897; Below: This is a modern rendition of one of Barnum's phony mermaids. Called the Fiji Mermaid, it was created by joining the bottom half of a fish with the top part of a mummified monkey.

His success confirmed that people often see what they want to see.

POSSIBLE EXPLANATIONS FOR MERMAID SIGHTINGS.

No one has proved the existence of mermaids. So then what did Columbus and others actually see? A more recent mermaid report might give us

a clue. In the mid-1980s, curious scientists traveled to Papua New Guinea (PAHP-yoo-uh noo GIN-ee), an island in the South Pacific Ocean, to see a mermaid-like creature they called a ri. Native witnesses claimed the ri had a humanlike torso and head. Disappointed researchers discovered that the creature was just a dugong (DOO-gawng)—an aquatic, plant-eating mammal, also called a sea cow.

A dugong (sea cow)

Another type of sea cow, the manatee, (MAN-uh-tee) may also have confused people in the past. The manatee is so homely that it's often considered adorable. Its fat, gray, torpedo-shaped body grows to about 12 feet (3.7 m) in length. It has a rounded tail and short, paddle-like front legs. The water mammal swims to the surface to breathe. When the manatee pokes its head out of the water, it reveals a face with small eyes, a deeply cleft upper lip, and big nostrils.

From a distance, could a manatee resemble a person? Did Columbus and his sailors think three manatees were mermaids? If so, it's easy to understand why the captain wrote, "They were not as beautiful as they are painted."

Chapter NINE

It's also possible that other animals could trick an observer's eyes. Perhaps a seal, bobbing in the waves or basking on a rock, could be mistaken for a human if seen from far away. Other animals that could be mistaken for mermaids are spy-hopping whales and walruses. Spy hopping occurs when an animal sticks its head up out of the water to glance around. Glimpsed from far off, it might look like a person surfacing. The sun's reflections on the water could add to a viewer's confusion by distorting objects.

Seals lying on a rock. From a distance, could they be mistaken for mermaids?

Die-hard believers insist that mermaids and mermen—or at least creatures that resemble them—do exist. Since water covers over 70 percent of our planet and we are still learning about what lurks in the ocean depths, they argue that mermaids could indeed exist somewhere in the vast seas. Marine biologists continue to find new life forms. Could the mermaid be a real sea creature that simply hasn't been captured and studied yet?

Just as mermaid stories have survived through the years, so, too, has the mystery surrounding a famous place that no one is sure actually ever existed.

CHAPTER TEN
⁓ The Lost Continent of Atlantis

Imagine what it would be like to live in a perfect place—
a "paradise on Earth." Books describe such places, but most people don't believe that they ever actually existed. One of these rumored paradises is the continent of Atlantis. Some people think Atlantis was real, but they can't prove it ever really existed. This is because the large island continent supposedly sank into the sea.

AN ANCIENT LEGEND

The first person to write about Atlantis was Plato, the Greek philosopher who lived around 400 B.C.—over 2,000 years ago. The story, which originally had been told by an elderly Egyptian priest, was passed down through Plato's family. Plato reported that Atlantis was home to an ancient civilization full of riches, whose people were highly advanced in their skills and knowledge. In the center of the capital city, a beautiful temple sat on a high hill. Its silver and gold trim glimmered in the sunlight, and its grounds were decorated with splendid golden statues of the kings and queens of Atlantis. High overhead, carved ivory covered the ceiling. Surrounding the temple were three rings of water, connected by canals.

On this old map from 1785, Atlantis is shown as being between Africa and South America.

⁓

Chapter TEN

Stone walls with tall watchtowers zigzagged across the continent's countryside. Paved roads connected ten cities, each ruled by its own king and queen. Gleaming white marble buildings stood throughout the land, and beautiful fountains bubbled both hot and cold water. Atlantis was blessed with animals, fruit and nut trees, lush gardens, and clear streams. Life was good.

Plato described the location of Atlantis as ". . .outside the Pillars of Hercules" (HER-kyuh-leez). This had always been thought to mean that the continent sat outside the Strait of Gibraltar (juh-BRAWL-ter), in the Atlantic Ocean. The Strait of Gibraltar lies between the continents of Europe and Africa and connects the Mediterranean Sea with the Atlantic Ocean.

Although Atlanteans were proud of their earthly paradise, they became greedy. Desiring even greater riches, they conquered other lands in their quest to rule the Mediterranean world. Then disaster struck. Violent earthquakes shook Atlantis, followed by killer floods. The island continent sank into the sea. It was as if it had never existed. . .and maybe it never had.

Did this really happen? Does evidence of a "lost" civilization lie someplace beneath the sea, or is the story a myth? In Plato's telling, the events took place nearly 12,000 years ago. But how could such an advanced civilization exist during a time when humans were still living in the Stone Age?

THE THEORIES SURROUNDING ATLANTIS

Ever since Plato first described Atlantis, people have debated its existence in thousands of books. In 1624, an English philosopher named Sir Francis Bacon wrote *The New Atlantis*. His story told about a country called Bensalem whose people had superhuman knowledge. They built structures a half-mile (.8 km) high, and even understood the principles of flight. The book increased interest in the original tale of Atlantis.

In 1882, a former United States Congressman, Ignatius Donnelly, wrote a popular book called *Atlantis: The Antediluvian World*. The word *antediluvian* (ANT-ee-dee-LOO-vee-en) means "ancient" and refers to the world as it was before the biblical flood. Donnelly believed that the Atlantis story, as told by Plato, was actual history, and that survivors from the doomed island migrated to Africa, Europe, and the Americas. According to Donnelly, the survivors from Atlantis influenced Aztec, Incan, and Mayan civilizations in the Americas. The cultures have many things in common: They play similar games, their artwork shows similarities, and their buildings, too, are much alike (pyramids, for example).

Some believers of Donnelly's theories go further. They think this "Survivors from Atlantis" theory explains how the Spanish explorer Cortes (kor-TEZ) defeated the Aztecs. Cortes had only about 500 Spanish soldiers when he landed in Mexico in 1519. Yet, within two years, he'd conquered the Aztecs who had tens of thousands of warriors. How did he do it?

The theory is that the Aztecs might have thought Cortes was a god. An ancient Aztec legend told of a tall bearded white man who would return from the East to take back his lands. This figure was considered a god; the Aztecs called him Quetzalcoatl (ket-SAHL-kwaht-ul). According to legend, Quetzalcoatl taught the Aztecs things such as astronomy, how to appreciate art, and how to avoid bad habits—knowledge that made them more civilized.

Cortes was a tall, bearded white man, so when he arrived, the Aztecs might have thought he was Quetzalcoatl. If that were the case, they wouldn't have viewed him or his men as enemies. This could have given the Spaniards time to figure out how to defeat the mighty Aztec warriors.

Was Quetzalcoatl a survivor of Atlantis? Long before the Spanish invasion, did this "god" from the lost continent pass along knowledge of math, science, and law to America's emerging civilization? Some researchers think it's possible. Others laugh at the idea.

Another novel appeared in 1870 that rekindled interest in Atlantis. Years before the modern submarine was invented, Jules Verne fascinated readers with his book, *20,000 Leagues Under the Sea*, in which the main character, Captain Nemo, cruises in a submarine-like vessel called the *Nautilus*. The captain and his crew are astonished by the wonders of an underwater city—a part of the lost continent of Atlantis. Years later the classic novel became a popular movie, again boosting interest in the missing island.

In the 1930s, people began hearing about Atlantis from an unusual source. Edgar Cayce was a clairvoyant (klayr-VOY-ent)—a person who reveals information about the future while in a hypnotic trance. Cayce correctly predicted some inventions and events before they happened, causing many people to believe he had special powers. During one of his trances, Cayce described the fate of Atlantis. Volcanic explosions set off the

The Mayan pyramid at Chichen Itza (above) and the Aztec pyramid at Teotihuacan (below), both in Mexico, show that the architecture of these two ancient cultures was very similar.

destruction, he said. Cayce predicted that the underwater ruins of Atlantis would be discovered near the Islands of the Bahamas. He said large crystals would be found within the ruins, and that the crystals were the source of a mysterious power held by the Atlanteans.

Drawing by Alphonse de Neuville from the book 20,000 Leagues Under the Sea. It shows an underwater volcano and the submerged city of Atlantis.

BELIEVERS AND SKEPTICS: WHAT BOTH SIDES SAY

Far-fetched? Not to some people. In the late 1960s, in the waters near Bimini, a small island in the Bahamas, divers found stone blocks that were originally part of an ancient road. Was the road on Atlantis? Scientists flocked to the site, and geologists took samples. Investigators declared that the "road" was a natural rock formation—it wasn't an Atlantis road after all.

Disappointed Atlantis-seekers refuse to give up. They think that proof of the continent's existence is hiding someplace in the Atlantic Ocean's deep waters. Their arguments are based mainly on strange animal behavior. For example:

◆ Some birds that migrate from Europe to South America each year circle over a particular area of the Atlantic Ocean. The birds act as if they're looking for land—for a resting place that no longer exists. After circling for a while, they continue their journey.

◆ Great masses of small rodents that live in Norway, called lemmings, swim out into the Atlantic Ocean. Do they expect to find land? They appear confused, swimming aimlessly until they drown.

◆ Eels from European rivers swim thousands of miles across the Atlantic Ocean to mate in the weedy waters of the Sargasso Sea. Do the eels travel so far because a lost continent once drew them to its shallow waters?

Biologists admit that these odd behaviors cannot be fully explained, but they don't think that the animals' instincts are connected to a continent that disappeared. Many scholars think that Atlantis is pure fantasy. They claim Plato was describing his own Greek civilization. He wanted to warn his fellow citizens that their greed and corruption could result in a terrible end to their society.

Nonbelievers also point out that no advanced civilization existed 12,000 years ago. Atlantis-believers accept this, but they have a simple explanation: They believe Plato's math was wrong—that his numbers were too large. They say that when the story was passed down, the Egyptian numeric symbols were misinterpreted. A simple correction would date the island's disappearance around 1500 B.C.—a time period when several advanced civilizations around the world existed. This date also coincides with an event that occurred on the tiny Greek island of Thera in the Aegean (ih-JEE-un) Sea—an island that some people believe is Plato's Atlantis.

Around 1470 B.C., most of Thera was destroyed when a massive volcanic eruption led to violent earthquakes. After the volcano's crater collapsed, huge tsunamis flooded parts of the island. This could explain Plato's claim that the continent was ". . .swallowed by the sea." Before the rising waters covered much of the island, Thera's shape was round. (Today, it's crescent-shaped and is called Santorini.)

Thera's advanced society had both recorded laws and engineering skills. Critics point out that the island couldn't be Atlantis because it isn't "outside the

After a volcano erupted on Thera, most of the island disappeared, leaving behind only a crescent-shaped section of the island.

Pillars of Hercules." But could it be that Plato wasn't describing the Straits of Gibraltar after all? Maybe he was writing about a place closer to Greece.

The arguments go on and on. Will the lost continent ever reveal itself? Did it exist or is it only a legend? Similar legends have proven to be true. The city of Troy, mentioned in Greek mythology, was assumed to be a fantasy. But then Troy was found and excavated in 1873, and historians were astonished.

Might Atlantis, like Troy, be found one day? Every time divers find evidence of an underwater city, Atlantis will be mentioned, and excitement will grow.

Chapter TEN

Aerial photo of Santorini today,
showing its crescent shape

Debates about Atlantis will continue. But there's little debate over what the scariest ocean predator is. Coming across this fish while swimming in the ocean is many people's worst nightmare. What is this frightening creature?

CHAPTER ELEVEN
Great White Ocean Terror

Gliding through the water like a torpedo, a great white shark closes in on an unsuspecting swimmer. Something causes the man to glance over his shoulder. His eyes widen in horror when he sees a triangle-shaped dorsal fin jutting through the water. Before the man even has time to react, the shark's sawlike teeth tear at his hip and upper leg, ripping out a large chunk of flesh. A shriek of terror fills the air. Then the shark attacks again, pulling the injured man under water.

We've seen horrifying scenes like this in movies and occasionally on the evening news. "Shark fever" took the world by storm in the mid 1970s after a popular book called *Jaws* became a record-smashing movie. The story of a vicious great white shark attacking swimmers was both fascinating and terrifying. Many people believed that something like this could really happen; others thought that fierce man-eating sharks didn't actually exist. In reality, recurring attacks like this are rare. Sharks don't usually hunt people. They prefer to dine on fish, seals, or sea lions.

However, this doesn't mean that shark attacks never occur. In the summer of 1916, over a period of about ten days, a shark (or sharks) terrorized the New Jersey coast, killing four people and injuring a fifth. When a 7-1/2 foot (2.3 m)

This shark, caught in July 1916, was believed to be one of the sharks terrorizing the Atlantic coast that summer. It measured 10 feet (3.1 m) and weighed 300 pounds (136.2 kg).

shark was finally caught and its stomach cut open, human bones and flesh were found inside.

SHARK CHARACTERISTICS

Simply hearing the word *shark* causes terror in many people. But each year, out of about 50 attacks total, sharks kill fewer than 10 people around the world. A person is more likely to be struck by lightning than bitten by a shark. So why do these fish frighten us? To answer this we must look at what makes the more than 350 species of sharks different from other fish in the seas.

Unlike fish with bony skeletons, a shark's skeleton is made of lightweight cartilage (KART-ul-ij)—the same

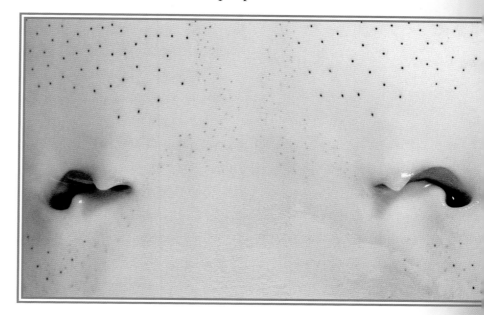

Close-up of the ampullae of Lorenzini on a shark's snout and chin

bendable material that shapes your nose and ears. Inside the shark's liver is oil. Because oil is lighter than water, it lessens the shark's weight in water and makes it more buoyant. Sharks have the same five senses that humans have: touch, smell, taste, sight, and sound. However, a shark's sense of smell is much stronger than a human's. This fish can smell a small amount of blood in the water nearly a mile away. A shark can also hear things that a person cannot. Because its inner ears are very sensitive to movement and vibration in the water, it can always tell when a meal is nearby. Sensory cells along the length of the shark's body also help it locate objects.

In addition to these traits, the shark is gifted with a sixth sense. Here's how it works. Animals moving in the water produce electrical currents. The weak electrical signals are picked up by small pores, called ampullae of the Lorenzini, on the shark's snout and chin. The pores connect to special cells inside the shark's body, which enable the shark to track and find the animal.

Shark feeding frenzy

There is one shark behavior in particular that sends chills down people's spines—the feeding frenzy. Thrashing sharks snap wildly at their food and even slash each other during a feeding frenzy. It's possible that this excited behavior is caused by overloaded senses, stimulated by the sudden appearance of a large meal for which many sharks are competing.

THE MOST FEARED FISH

In the 1940s, during World War II, nightmarish stories circulated about sailors who had been stranded in the ocean after their ships had been sunk by enemy fire. The stories said that dozens of sharks swarmed to areas where the sailors were, most likely attracted by the men's frantic splashing and by the blood from their injuries.

Sharks are constantly on the lookout for signs of weakness in their prey. This is actually helpful behavior because it keeps the oceans healthy and free of sick or wounded fish and animals that might infect other sea creatures. A diver at a park in California had this experience:

> I was underwater with an eight-foot long (2.4-m) female shark. I was cleaning her tank, like I'd done before. Suddenly the shark gripped my head in her mouth and violently shook me. My first instinct was to punch her. To my relief, she let go and swam away. I got out of there in a hurry. Later I concluded I'd been attacked because I was wearing a wetsuit with a rip in the hood's outer material. Sharks can see colors, and the red lining on the underneath side of the hood made it look like I had an open wound. By hitting the shark I proved I was healthy, not weak and wounded. Luckily, I only suffered a bad headache and a case of jangled nerves.

Of all of the world's shark species, the great white is the most feared. In some places they are called "white death." Regarded as man-eaters, great whites can be recognized by their long snouts, white bellies, and gray backs. Their eyes are round and black. And surprisingly, considering it is one of the most well-known types of shark, the great white is one of the rarest. Uncommon in tropical seas, it prefers cooler waters.

We tend to make monsters out of creatures we don't understand, and the great white is a species about which we know very little. Marine biologists haven't been able to study them closely because it's not easy keeping the sharks alive in captivity. When put into tanks, the sharks usually act confused and refuse to eat. They bump into the sides of the tanks, stop swimming, and soon die.

WHAT IS AND ISN'T KNOWN ABOUT SHARKS?

Many things aren't known about great whites, such as how long they live, how often and how much they eat, how many exist in our oceans, whether or not they migrate, and if they do, where they go. These are just a few of the unanswered questions.

HUMANS: THE SHARK'S GREATEST ENEMY

Each year millions of sharks of all types are killed by humans—some for food, others for sport. Finning—a practice that is common elsewhere in the world—is illegal in the United States. Finning occurs when commercial fishermen catch sharks, cut off their fins, and throw the bodies back into the sea, leaving the sharks to bleed to death. Fishermen can earn a lot of money selling the fins, which are used to make shark-fin soup—a gourmet dish in some parts of the world.

Hundreds of cutoff shark fins and pieces of shark meat

Sharks aren't killed just for their fins, however. Other shark parts are used in a variety of products. Sharkskin is made into belts and shoes. Shark liver oil is an ingredient that's sometimes added to makeup, medicine, and paint. There is great demand for the jaws of great whites; some people like to show them off as trophies. This could lead to the great white shark's becoming an endangered species. Some countries have made shark hunting illegal, but most others still allow it.

Many people think of great white sharks as mindless killing machines and wonder why we should bother protecting them. Is the great white's bad reputation fair? Not really. To put it into perspective, sharks wouldn't even make the list of the top ten dangers you need to worry about. But human beings would certainly be near the top of the list of dangers to a shark.

Divers on scientific expeditions have spent hours under water, suspended in protective cages, observing and filming the great white shark. The sharks have proven to be curious but careful when dealing with humans. One diver described his experience:

Chapter ELEVEN

I was submerged inside a cylinder-shaped clear plastic cage. The cage was made of a strong material used in bulletproof windows, giving a great 360 degree view of underwater activity. I'd been filming two great white sharks for half an hour. From time to time they approached my nearly-invisible cage, not showing aggression, but merely curious about me and the air bubbles rising from my tank. When the sharks' snouts bumped into the cage, the sounds were like squeegees against the plastic. Soon one of the sharks disappeared, but the other one—an 11-foot (3.3 m) female—suddenly hovered nose-to-nose with me, separated only by my transparent plastic cylinder. The shark lingered for a full 20 seconds, staring at me, as if trying to determine just what a human really was.

The jaws of a great white shark are for sale at this shop.

The more researchers watch and learn about great white sharks, the more they admire these ocean predators and worry about their future. As people learn that great whites aren't the vicious human-killers they thought they were, fear is replaced with respect.

Sharks' immune systems intrigue scientists, who wonder how sharks are able to eat diseased fish and animals without becoming ill themselves. Scientists hope that by studying sharks, we may come to a better understanding of our own diseases and immune systems. It would be ironic if one of the creatures most hated and feared by people led scientists to the cure for some human diseases.

We're awed by the great white shark's power. Many people think the great white is the most frightening animal on our planet. The fact that we don't know much about this fish adds to the fear and mystery. But what's certain is that its survival depends on our actions. We must put our hatred and fear aside and protect the great white from extinction.

IF YOU WANT TO LEARN MORE

Tsunami   http://www.pmel.noaa.gov/tsunami

Bermuda Triangle   http://www.history.navy.mil/faqs/faq8-1.htm

Sargasso Sea   http://va.essortment.com/sargassoseawid_ramo.htm

The Atocha   http://www.melfisher.com

Giant Squid   http://seawifs.gsfc.nasa.gov/squid.html

Leech   http://animaldiversity.ummz.umich.edu/site/accounts/information/Hirudo_medicinalis.html

Loch Ness Monster   http://www.nessie.co.uk/

Niagara Falls   http://www.niagarafallsstatepark.com

Mermaid   http://rubens.anu.edu.au/student.projects/mermaids/homepage.html

Atlantis   http://en.wikipedia.org/wiki/Atlantis

Great White Shark   http://www.enchantedlearning.com/subjects/sharks/species/Greatwhite.shtml

GLOSSARY

ampulla of Lorenzini small pores on a shark's snout and chin that pick up the weak electronic signals given off by other animals, letting the shark know what other animals are around

annelid any type of worm with a long, segmented body

antediluvian from or referring to the time before the flood that's described in the Bible

asthenosphere part of the earth's interior that is made up of molten rock

becalmed when a ship isn't moving due to lack of wind

bloodletting old practice whereby some of a sick person's blood was drained to try to heal the person

buoyant capable of floating

cartilage bendable material that makes up a shark's skeleton, and that is also found in a person's ear and tip of the nose

cascade steep, small waterfall

cataract large waterfall

cephalopods any type of mollusk (an animal with a soft, boneless body) with muscular arms around its head that usually have suckers on them, like squids and octopuses

Glossary

clairvoyant person who is able to see into the past or the future and sense things others cannot

compass variation the difference between magnetic north, which is the direction the earth's northern axis point faces, and true north

dugong aquatic, plant-eating mammal that's related to the manatee; also called a sea cow

eddy current of water that's moving or spinning in the opposite direction of the main current

galleon large sailing ship used from the fifteenth to the seventeenth century especially by Spanish merchants or as a warship

hirudin chemical that prevents blood from clotting

lemming small mouselike, short-tailed rodent that lives in northern climates

mailbox L-shaped tube that fits over a boat's propeller; blasts of water through the tube make craters in the sand of the sea floor, uncovering any treasure that might hidden underneath

manatee aquatic, plant-eating mammal with paddlelike front flippers and a flat tail

manifest list of the cargo (items) or passengers carried on a ship or plane

mantle soft, loose layer that covers a giant squid's body

microburst sudden, strong downdraft of air over a small area

peat partially rotted plant matter, usually mosses, found in the water

plesiosaur large, extinct marine reptile common in Europe and North America during the Mesozoic Era

Richter Scale scale from 1 to 10 expressing the total amount of energy given off by an earthquake

sterncastle rear area of old ships where the captain and wealthy passengers would stay

tectonic plates layers of the earth's crust that move and float, and sometimes collide with one another, causing earthquakes, volcanoes, or the formation of mountain ranges

waterspout funnel-shaped tornado that forms over the water and that is made up of air and water spray

INDEX